"*Aspire* is a must read for any leader who aspires to greatness."

—Alice Elliot, president and CEO, The Elliot Group

"Kevin Hall's message of personal growth and focused purpose echo the outlook of Sir Henry Royce, co-founder of Rolls-Royce Motor Cars, who famously said, 'Strive for perfection in everything you do. Take the best that exists and make it better.' *Aspire* is making the best even better."

—Peter Miles, executive vice president, BMW North America, and former president, Rolls-Royce Motor Cars North America

"What an incredible book. I felt like I was on a journey the whole time I was reading it. I just gave out ten copies to close friends and associates."

—Joan Linton, co-founder, School Improvement Network

"This revealing book takes you on a journey of discovery filled with recurring 'wows' and 'aha's!' Uncovering the true meaning of a core word is like turning on a light switch. *Aspire* should be broadly read and generously shared."

—Jon L. Luther, chairman, Dunkin' Brands

"I can't wait to see the world's response to *Aspire*. It's so rich, and so rewarding, that it deserves to be read repeatedly."

—John Assaraf, *New York Times* bestselling author of *The Answer,* and teacher in *The Secret*

Aspire

DISCOVERING YOUR PURPOSE
THROUGH THE POWER OF WORDS

KEVIN HALL

WILLIAM MORROW

An Imprint of HarperCollins*Publishers*

This book was originally published by Bookwise Publishing in 2009.

HarperCollins books may be purchased for educational, business, or
sales promotional use. For information, please e-mail the Special
Markets Department at SPsales@harpercollins.com.

First William Morrow hardcover edition published 2010.

Title design by Iskra
Book design by Francine Eden Platt, Eden Graphics
Photo by John Neal Crossman

Library of Congress Cataloging-in-Publication Data

Hall, Kevin.
    Aspire: discovering your purpose through the power of words /
Kevin Hall. —1st ed.
        p.   cm.
    ISBN 978-0-06-196454-1
    1. English language—Semantics. 2. English language—Spoken
English. 3. English language—Written English. 4. Written
communication. 5. Oral communication. 6. Vocabulary. I. Title.
    PE1585.H323 2010
    420.1' 43—dc22

                                                      2009039209

17 OV/RRD 10 9

This book is dedicated to the undisputed Master of Words,
Professor Arthur Watkins.

I will be forever grateful that you appeared on my path.

Contents

ForeWord – *by Stephen R. Covey*   *ix*

Author's Note   *xv*

Chapter One – The Secret Word   *1*

Chapter Two – Pathfinder   *19*

Chapter Three – Namasté   *39*

Chapter Four – Passion   *63*

Chapter Five – Sapere Vedere   *87*

Chapter Six – Humility   *109*

Chapter Seven – Inspire   *125*

Chapter Eight – Empathy   *145*

Chapter Nine – Coach   *163*

Chapter Ten – Ollin   *183*

Chapter Eleven – Integrity   *205*

The Book of Greats   *229*

AfterWord – *by Dr. Gerald Bell*   *236*

ForeWord

It all started with words. In John 1:1 we read, "In the beginning was the Word, and the Word was with God. And the Word was God." Words are, and always have been, the creative force of the universe. The first recorded words of the Creator, "Let there be light," put forth the illuminating power of words.

This masterfully written book will help you understand that words contain an inherent power, a force capable of lighting one's paths and hoped-for horizons. Used correctly and positively, words are the first building blocks for success and inner peace; they provide the vision and focus that show the way to growth and contribution. Used incorrectly and negatively, they are capable of undermining even the best of intentions. This is true in business, in personal relationships, and in every other walk of life. There is a language of success and a language of distress. There is a language of progress and a language of regress. Words sell, and words repel. Words lead, and words impede. Words heal, and words kill. By truly understanding what words mean in their purest sense, we are able to unlock their importance and divine value and put ourselves in position to develop a new leadership vocabulary that looks up, not down, and inspires, motivates, uplifts, excites, and propels. When words are used properly, they sing out to the human heart.

ABOUT YOUR PATHFINDER

I first met Kevin Hall over two decades ago when he was leading the sales and training division at Franklin Quest. He requested that I speak at the corporation's annual retreat on the principles of communication and empathy. His passion for timeless principles and sincere desire to help others find and follow their path and purpose in life were clearly evident back then.

Kevin was also the coach for my granddaughter Lauren's club soccer team, where I was able to observe his ability to motivate and encourage young people to achieve goals many of them had never dreamed of. He was as concerned with the players' personal success in life as he was with their success on the soccer field. I remember one occasion in particular when we opened up our home for a personal development session for team members, and Kevin arranged for a handful of speakers to "breathe life" into the players' dreams and aspirations. One speaker, Art Berg, shared a powerful message you will read about in Chapter 7. Many of the principles taught that night still resonate with me even today.

Over time, the company I founded, Covey Leadership Center, merged with Franklin Quest to form FranklinCovey, a leading global professional services firm of which I serve as vice chairman today.

Prior to the merger, Kevin left Franklin Quest to pursue the founding of a youth foundation and research the hidden, and often secret, meaning of words, as well as their relationship to personal growth and development.

We have since spoken together at industry conferences and worked jointly with executive teams in improving leadership performance. Just as I broke new ground in human development over twenty years ago by uncovering the habits that make for a meaningful and effective life, Kevin is breaking new ground by uncovering and revealing the true intent and meaning of the words that make up those habits.

I have been conferring with Kevin on this book over the course of the past four years and believe it to be a magnificent guide for living a life of fulfillment and integrity. Each chapter is infused with timeless principles that Kevin calls "secrets." For example, in Chapter 1, you will discover the Secret Word. It is an ancient and incredibly empowering word from India that I have personally found to be amazingly potential-releasing. Discovering this word alone, and learning how to tap into its illimitable power, is more than worth the price of the book.

As you read about Kevin's personal journey of discovering these secrets, you'll soon come to realize the power of your own heroic journey.

PEELING THE ONION

Understanding what a common word really means and recognizing its depth and true essence can be enormously empowering. By breaking down words, layer by layer, by uncovering their pure, original meaning, by exploring their roots, we shine a new light on words and phrases, many of which we've used forever. For example,

I have always taught that the first imperative of a leader is to inspire others. When you realize that "inspire" means *to breathe life into another's dreams,* and that the opposite, "expire," means *to cease to breathe,* those words come to life. By learning to use words that inspire, you enable others to achieve their dreams. Conversely, by using words that expire, you disable others' hopes and aspirations.

Another example is "opportunity." I believe that effective people are not problem-minded; they're opportunity-minded. The root of opportunity is *port,* meaning the entryway by water into a city or place of business. In earlier days, when the tide and winds were right and the port opened, it allowed entry to do commerce, to visit, or to invade and conquer. But only those who recognized the opening could take advantage of the open port, or opportunity. I strongly encourage you to take advantage of the opportunity this treasure-filled book affords for enriching your life.

In addition to words commonly used in everyday English conversation, this book includes unique and profound words from other languages and cultures. The word "Ollin," for example, is a word of depth from the Aztecs. It described a powerful event, like an earthquake or a great storm that shakes the earth. It conveys intense and immediate movement. Ollin means *to move or act now with all your heart.* To experience Ollin, you have to get "All in." Global words such as this can unite people throughout the world with a common language.

FINDING YOUR BLISS

The more you understand words and the layers within them, the more it helps you understand your path and purpose. The great mythologist Joseph Campbell coined the phrase "Follow your bliss." Words are the direction signs that show the way to that bliss. Words, in concert with the actions they inspire, help you become a better leader, a better spouse, a better parent, a better salesperson, a better athlete. The list is endless. The power in words generates wealth, health, productivity, discipline, spirituality, and limitless other desirable human traits.

LAYOUT OF THE CHAPTERS

By design, the book is divided into eleven principle-based chapters—eleven core words—that you can visit and revisit several times a year to effectively cement permanent behavioral change.

The pattern and layout of the chapters reflect the author's background and experience in human development training over the past quarter century. The first five chapters deal with personal development—how to use the secret power of words to help find your personal path and purpose. The middle chapter sits by itself, deliberately set apart because its theme is central to the whole book. Its key word is "humility," a powerful trait I regard as the "Mother of all Virtues," for it is the key to growth and constant improvement. The last five chapters are about leading others. They comprise the language of leadership: *it's not about you, it's about them.*

As in a wheel, the chapters reflect how your sphere of influence expands from an inner hub, then gets bigger and bigger and bigger as the wheel keeps growing. The final chapter on "integrity"—which means *whole* or *complete*—completes the development wheel.

This enlightening book can easily be read in a single sitting. You can also select a chapter theme that calls to you and explore its depths thoroughly and deliberately. Either way, it will reveal essential keys for unleashing your true potential.

Whatever your goal, your quest, your passion, I am confident *Aspire* will unlock for you a universal force that will light the way to inspiration and personal growth. I suggest you keep a pen or pencil close by as you read this profound work over and over again. I know I will.

— STEPHEN R. COVEY

Author's Note

As I finished this manuscript today, a fresh blanket of snow covered the mountaintop community where I live. I stepped outside and took in a deep breath of fresh air, and slowly exhaled. The painfully sweet work of the previous four years seemed to evaporate like the steam rising from my breath. As I've repeated to myself, during several epic Leadville 100 mountain bike races, I thought: *The pain is soon forgotten but the memory of the victory lives on forever.*

If this book brings value and meaning into but one life, it will have been more than worth the countless hours invested in it. As a connector of ideas and people, I doubt someone could pay me enough money to abandon this work and not pass along the secrets that I discovered while on my journey in writing *Aspire*.

It is my hope that you will discover value in the principles I've learned and find fulfillment and happiness as you apply them in your life. It is also my desire that you will seize the opportunity provided at the end of each chapter, and in "The Book of Greats" section at the conclusion of this book, to honor key individuals who have enriched your life. Dr. Martin E. P. Seligman, a world-renowned authority in the field of positive psychology and the bestselling author of *Learned Optimism* and *Authentic Happiness,* teaches that we can achieve new levels of happiness by reaching out and thanking those who have made a positive impact on our lives. These "gratitude visits" have been scientifically proven to be the No. 1 way to promote personal happiness. I promise that if you try it, you will like it, and so will those you are recognizing.

As your personal journey continues to unfold, I would very much enjoy learning about your unique experiences. By combining our energies, we will help each other stay on our path, keep our commitments, and fulfill our purpose. **Please feel free to correspond with me at kevin@ powerofwords.com.** I look forward to hearing from you.

— KEVIN HALL

CHAPTER ONE

The Secret Word

If I have no other qualities I can succeed with love alone. Without it I will fail though I possess all the knowledge and skills of the world. I will greet this day with love in my heart.

— Og Mandino —

It was a cold, brisk winter afternoon as I stepped inside the majestic St. Stephen's Cathedral, positioned at the very focal point of picturesque Vienna, Austria.

I found myself instantly drawn to a simple framed photograph of a young Mother Teresa surrounded by candles and benches. I silently reflected on the impact of this tiny woman's large life, a megadoer of few "words," who changed the world by doing one good deed after another and was known to whisper "Don't talk; just do" long before Nike's "Just do it" slogan came about.

Mother Teresa, who never bore children of her own, became the mother of the motherless by adhering to a mantra of "doing little things with great love." "Doing." "Acting." "Serving." Those words became her calling cards to the world.

I left the cathedral inspired by her legacy and committed to "do more doing." Surrounded by the magnificent spires of St. Stephen's, I aspired to reach higher and reevaluate and recognize the opportunities along my path. I had a reassuring feeling that something special was about to happen.

I then remembered why I had walked in that direction

to begin with and began looking for Christmas gifts for my loved ones back home. I began searching the alleys and side streets, passing the many gift shops and sidewalk cafés, in search of something special. Walking the cobbled steps from the cathedral, I paused in front of a store with a window display that reminded me of a jewelry box, only it was a fabric shop.

The light reflecting off the luminous silks and colorful linens caught my eye and tugged at my heart. I entered the store in hopes of finding the perfect fabric for my daughter Season's wedding dress. As I surveyed the colorful buffet of materials gathered from every corner of the world, I envisioned my daughter looking like a princess, radiating her beautiful smile and infectious laugh while her Prince Charming carried her across a new threshold of promise and hope.

I was completely unaware that the path I was following would lead to the discovery of one of the most meaningful gifts of my life.

This gift would come packaged in the form of a word, a word with the power to transform one's life forever.

An Unexpected Gift

The middle-aged proprietor of the store leaped toward me with the bounding energy of someone half his age. He offered his hand in welcome. I was completely taken by his large brown eyes. His face was round, and his pearl white teeth accentuated his smooth, chocolate-colored skin.

As he shook my hand, he smiled with a subtle wink,

tilted his head, and said in proper and precise English, "Good evening. My name is Pravin. Pravin Cherkoori." His voice had the disarming soft intonation of one who had come from the country of his store's name: India.

"I'm Kevin Hall. I'm pleased to meet you," I replied.

I was about to ask how long he had been acquiring the brilliant array of colors and fabrics that dazzled the eye, when to my surprise he had a question for me.

"What is that pin you are wearing?" he inquired.

I touched the pewter pin on the lapel of my overcoat. I removed it and offered it to him for a closer look. He took it between his thumb and index finger and asked, "What do the two hands clasped at each wrist represent?"

"They depict our responsibility to reach out, uplift one another, and lighten one another's burdens," I answered.

Pravin rotated the pin one half turn and said, "It looks as if both hands are equally positioned to either help or be helped."

"You obviously understand what the artist was trying to convey," I responded. "Emerson called it 'one of the beautiful compensations of this life, for you cannot sincerely try to help another without helping yourself.'"

His smile made the corners of his mouth curve upward as he added, "We often receive what we desire for others."

I nodded because his words rang true.

"So this pin . . . this is why you are here in Vienna?" Pravin queried.

I was surprised he made the connection but I didn't comment. I explained that the pin is a miniature replica of the Statue of Responsibility that Viktor Frankl envisioned being built on the West Coast of America as a bookend monument to the Statue of Liberty on the East Coast. I'd spent the past week with Viktor's family, showing them this model and discussing plans to fulfill his vision.

The shopkeeper's eyes widened at the mention of the name of the famed Viennese psychiatrist, Holocaust survivor, and author of *Man's Search for Meaning*. "I knew Viktor. He was a great and noble man," Pravin said with admiration, at which point he reached beneath the front counter and produced a large leather guest book. "Viktor, like many others who have passed through Vienna, signed this Book of Greats."

He leaned forward as he opened the book and placed it on top of the counter directly in front of me and said, "Kevin, you are one of the greats. Will you sign my book?"

I looked at the names on the pages. There was Dr. Frankl, and Mother Teresa, and members of Mahatma Gandhi's family. *This man has just met me,* I thought. I felt unworthy of signing his book. Certainly my name didn't belong alongside such distinguished company.

After pausing for what seemed an eternity, I responded, "I appreciate the compliment and your thoughtful gesture, but I do not believe that I am one of the greats. I'm sorry, but I can't sign your book."

Pravin came around the counter and placed his hand on my shoulder. "I have a word I wish to teach you," he said. "Would you be so kind as to join me for dinner?"

Without waiting for my reply, he led me out the front door, where the cold air was a chilly reminder that growth and discovery are often accompanied by a degree or two of discomfort.

After a series of turns and bends, we followed the sweet scent of stir-fried vegetables, roasted garlic, and ginger to a quaint Chinese restaurant.

The décor of the restaurant was plain and simple. Dull gray walls encompassed eight small rectangular dining tables, each nestled with four wooden chairs, all perched atop a dingy vinyl floor. The partially visible kitchen revealed a six-burner stove, overcrowded with iron woks, steel sauce pans, and stock pots. An assortment of metal utensils hung from the stainless steel hood above the stove. The counter to the left held stacks of oval serving dishes. The open shelf above was loaded to the brim with white-and-red takeout containers.

We arrived in the early evening, between the rush of lunch and dinner, and discovered we had the dining room all to ourselves.

One cook was skillfully slicing and chopping vegetables in preparation for the inevitable crowds of the night, while a second cook artfully prepared a meal-to-go with a flaming wok in his right hand. He stood in front of the stove with his back to us, and like an orchestra conductor, he moved his arms rhythmically, as if to the beat of a stunning symphony.

This unusual setting framed the extraordinary encounter that ensued. Here, in a Chinese restaurant in the center of Europe, a conversation took flight as if it were on the wings of angels, between complete strangers who confided in each other as if they were lifelong friends.

Pravin, eager to get to the business at hand, called the waitress over and quickly ordered a few of his favorite dishes. He then scooted forward on his chair and placed his elbows on the table in front of me. Looking me directly in the eyes, he asked, "What do you believe about me? I am dark-skinned. You are light-skinned. I am from the East. You are from the West. What do we have in common?"

I didn't need to think long about my response. Words my mother taught me since I was a child echoed in my mind. Without hesitating, I replied, "I believe that you are my brother. We were created by the same Creator. We are part of the same human family."

My Indian brother relaxed back in his chair and exclaimed, "That is what I believe also!"

From that moment on our conversation took on a depth of personal interest as if we had broken new ground and understanding.

Pravin spoke about his early years. "I grew up in Calcutta," he began, "among the poorest of the poor. Through education and hard work my family was able to break the shackles of poverty." After a pause, he resumed. "My mother taught me many great things. One of the most important was the meaning of an ancient Hindi word."

That brought me to the edge of my chair.

"In the West you might call this charity," Pravin went on. "But I think you'll find this word has a deeper meaning."

What word could have more depth than charity? I thought.

Speaking deliberately, almost reverently, he continued as if he were revealing a sacred secret.

"The word is 'Genshai,'" he said. "It means that you should never treat another person in a manner that would make them feel small."

I pulled out my leather journal and wrote the salient word "Genshai" (pronounced GEN-shy) and its meaning as taught by my newfound friend.

Pravin continued, "As children, we were taught to never look at, touch, or address another person in a way that would make them feel small. If I were to walk by a beggar in the street and casually toss him a coin, I would not be practicing Genshai. But if I knelt down on my knees and looked him in the eye when I placed that coin in his hand, that coin became love. Then and only then, after I had exhibited pure, unconditional brotherly love, would I become a true practitioner of Genshai."

Chills ran up and down my spine as I sat speechless, reflecting on the power of what I had just heard.

"Kevin, you are truly one of the greats," my host proclaimed, as he motioned toward me with his hands. "But you refused to sign my Book of Greats. When you made that decision, you treated yourself small. Genshai means that you never treat anyone small—and that includes yourself!"

He paused, then implored, "Promise me this, Kevin. Promise me that you will never, ever treat yourself small again. Will you do that for me?"

I felt humbled and surrendered. "I will, Pravin. I promise you, I will."

An inaudible *mission accomplished* seemed to dance across Pravin's beaming face as he sat back smiling from ear to ear.

A MOTHER'S LOVE

Just hours earlier, I had left the cathedral with a premonition that tonight would be memorable. As I glanced over at my guru-like guide, "memorable" seemed to be the biggest one-word understatement of the year.

"Pravin, can you tell me more about meeting Mother Teresa, the Saint of Calcutta?"

"Yes," he began. "She was walking through a throng of people dressed in her familiar white cotton sari. I raced in her direction, shouting and screaming, and as I ran up close to her, she reached out and placed her hand over my mouth and firmly beseeched me to 'stop talking and start doing.' I remember it as if it were—"

"It was Mother Teresa who brought me to your very street tonight," I interrupted, unable to contain my excitement. "A short while ago I stopped at St. Stephen's Cathedral and paid homage to her life. I left vowing to aspire to do more in my life. My next stop turned out to be your beautiful fabric store."

Pravin paused, looked intently into my eyes, and boldly said, "Our paths were meant to cross. We were destined to meet. You entered my shop for a reason."

I looked into the eyes of my new friend and was reminded of my own mother, who was the first to model

Genshai to me, although I'm positive she never heard the word nor knew of its meaning. "Kevin," she would say as she lifted my chin, "you can do anything that you want in life. You can achieve and live every worthwhile dream. You will surely do great and meaningful things in your life."

As I reflected on my childhood, the words were as clear then as the day she said them. It was almost as if the empty chair next to Pravin at our table was now peacefully occupied by my maternal angel.

It had been four years since my beautiful mother had passed away peacefully at our home. For nearly a year she valiantly fought the ravages of cancer, finally calmly and serenely surrendering.

To my family, to me, and to those who truly knew her, she will always be remembered as a remarkably strong and courageous woman.

She became a single mother of two at the tender age of nineteen, attending to the needs of my older brother and me when she could have been in her first year of college.

She was a teenage high-school dropout who leveraged self-education, career training, and sheer determination to become a substance abuse counselor right alongside colleagues with master's degrees hanging on their walls.

A recovered alcoholic, she had come full circle to counsel and comfort addicts who battled the same demons she knew all too well. Her challenges taught her how to understand others and empathize with their struggles and disappointments, and through it all she learned the value of compassion and encouragement—the foundational elements of Genshai.

At her funeral a tall, strong-looking, handsome man approached me with misty eyes and told me that my mother had changed and probably saved his life. He recounted a time when he was at the darkest point of his life. He had hit rock bottom and wasn't sure if he would ever get up again. Then, with tears streaming down his cheeks, he told me how she had believed in him when he didn't believe in himself. "Without your mother's help," he cried, "I wouldn't be here today."

Without her, I remembered thinking, *I wouldn't be here either,* for she had consistently declared to me that I could accomplish *anything* I set my mind to achieve, and fortunately I believed her. No matter how hard life became for her, she always held a view of a much better world for me.

A VICTOR, NOT A VICTIM

As we left the restaurant, my thoughts turned to another exemplar of Genshai, a man of extraordinary character and resilience, a man whose legacy had brought me to Vienna: Dr. Viktor Frankl.

One short week ago, I had left the warm confines of sunny Southern California to journey halfway around the globe with one hope in mind: the hope of learning more about Viktor's remarkable life and understanding how so much good could have come out of so much bad.

I began my course of study by walking the very same streets that Viktor had walked for all but three of the ninety-two years of his dignified and purpose-filled life.

The young doctor would spend those other three years far removed from the beauty and tranquility of his beloved Vienna, surviving the horrors and inhumanity of the Nazi concentration camps as prisoner Number 119,104.

To him, those three stolen years paled in comparison to what else the Nazis would take away and destroy: his beautiful bride and unborn child, his brother, his mother, his father, and the manuscript he had devoted his adult life to writing.

I will not forget how I felt as I stood outside the Frankl home, picturing the Nazis coming in the dark silence of the night and turning his haven into his hell, snatching Viktor and his loved ones from their warm beds to send them off in cattle trains to the concentration camps.

How could one choose to be victorious in the midst of such heartbreak and devastation? How could he choose triumph over defeat? Would I be able to approach that kind of courage?

How could Viktor, like Anne Frank, choose to believe in the goodness of mankind after what he had experienced?

Those answers are in the book that he wrote in nine successive days after his ordeal had ended, a book that would be recognized as one of the most influential books ever written: *Man's Search for Meaning*.

In the book he writes: "Everything can be taken from a man but one thing: the last of the human freedoms—to choose one's attitude in any given set of circumstances, to choose one's own way."

Despite his circumstances, he chose meaning, responsibility, and contribution. By choosing to be "worthy of his suffering," he proved that we each have the capacity to rise above our outward fate by walking the dignified path.

Stripped of possessions, every familiar piece of life snatched away, everything of value or worth destroyed; dehumanized and treated as if he were the smallest of the small; forced to suffer pain, hunger, thirst, fatigue, almost more than one can suffer without dying: the man who had become a *number* became a *person*.

Viktor, aptly named, chose to be a *victor,* not a *victim.* He discovered humanity in the empty face of inhumanity; he found hope amid a vast sea of hopelessness. In the face of overwhelming resistance he refused to treat himself, or others, small.

Words Light the Path

As Pravin and I retraced our steps toward his shop, I told him about my daughter and her wedding. He suggested we go back to the store, where he wrapped three exquisite silk and lace fabrics. After I thanked him, an awkward silence prevailed as we left the store. Our echoing footsteps were the only sound as we walked the centuries-old cobblestoned streets.

We stopped at a crossroads. In one direction was Pravin's home; in the other, my hotel.

Poised to go our separate ways, Pravin stepped forward and removed the scarf from around his neck and placed it around mine. He then gently tucked it inside my coat, where it felt as if it were warming my heart.

As we hugged goodbye, Pravin's last words were "It is all a journey, Kevin. We are all on a journey."

I turned and with a quick wave walked away, reflecting on what I had just learned. The lesson I learned was profound yet simple. *One word could change the world for the better.* Words are like passwords. They unlock the power. They open the door. Genshai. That single word contained as much depth as any lesson or sermon I had ever heard.

I will be forever grateful for the wise guide who helped me recall vividly my mother's message and at a deeper level understand what words are capable of. I vowed to never again treat myself small, to live Genshai, and to share this and other secret words, for it has been wisely said, "He who holds a lantern to light the pathway of his brother sees more clearly his own."

As I continued on my path, holding the package for my daughter, I realized that the Book of Greats has many empty pages to fill, and that one day I would return here again.

Now I had the light, and the direction I needed to take was clearer than ever before. I had come to Vienna to help others and yet had received the greatest gift. I glanced down at the package and smiled—well, two very special gifts.

Pravin was right. It is all a journey. We are all on a journey filled with gifts.

MY JOURNAL THOUGHTS ON *Genshai*

The way I treat myself reflects the way I treat others.

When I treat myself with dignity and respect, it will be reflected in the way I treat others. If I treat myself with disdain and contempt, that will be reflected in the way I treat others.

I don't see the world as it is. I see the world as I see myself.

Remember what James Allen wrote in As a Man Thinketh:

"Man is made or unmade by himself; in the armory of thought he forges the weapons by which he destroys himself. He also fashions the tools with which he builds for himself heavenly mansions of joy and strength and peace."

I have divinity within me . . . I have greatness within me . . . I attract into my life that which I believe I am.

"Believe" means to be love. When I believe in myself, I love myself. When I love myself, I treat myself with respect. "spect" is to look at. "Re" is back. "Respect" is to look back at.

I will write the secret word _Genshai_ on a piece of paper and put it on the bathroom mirror. Each day I will look in the mirror with love, honor, and respect. From this day on I will commit to living a magical, extraordinary life.

Abundance is my birthright. I need to think abundantly. It's time to release the potential within. It's time to begin my own heroic journey.

As I reflect Genshai to myself, the world will reflect it back.

IDENTIFY AND HONOR A PRACTITIONER OF
Genshai

SELECT someone whose behavior best reflects the principles of Genshai.

WRITE that person's name in the box provided below.

REACH OUT to and teach that person the meaning of "Genshai" and explain why he or she personifies this word.

CHAPTER TWO

PATHFINDER

The moment one definitely commits oneself then Providence moves too. All sorts of things occur to help one that would never otherwise have occurred . . . unforeseen incidents, meetings, and material assistance which no man could have dreamed would have come his way.

— WILLIAM HUTCHINSON MURRAY —

I t is the last day of the year.

The final hours of the year are approaching as I am at my desk, high in the Rocky Mountains, looking north out of a picture window that frames the beautiful snow-capped Wasatch Range, encircling the valley below as if it were a giant horseshoe.

In this elevated community suitably named Suncrest, our home is perched atop an alpine setting 6,000 feet up. Here, the sun crests over our mountaintop haven at the first light of day.

As the sun's eye slowly opens over the grandeur of Lone Peak to the east, I am reading *The Pilgrimage,* by my Brazilian friend Paulo Coehlo. What he writes triggers a torrential downpour of fresh insights, confirming to me the wisdom of always having two books with you: the book you are reading and the book you are writing. Placing pen to paper, I write fast and feverishly in my leather journal, barely able to write and contain the abundance of ideas.

My thoughts are interrupted by an explosion of fireworks streaming across the sky, changing the clouds from amber to burnt orange to blazing red. As the color bursts through the clouds, thin rays of light reach to the horizon like giant eyelashes, releasing life-sustaining energy to the new day.

Today's bright beginning will mark the ending of the year, for tonight when the clock strikes midnight we will bid adieu to the year gone by and welcome the New Year. Tomorrow at sunrise the earth begins anew its 365-day journey around the sun, demonstrating the connectivity of all things in the universe.

The words of William Wordsworth, "Come forth into the light of things, let Nature be your teacher," call out to me, and I reflect on a day last summer when my son Konnor and I, along with several other fathers and sons, stood in the enormous glacial cirque at the base of Lone Peak, the tallest of the tall peaks above Suncrest. There, the rock-littered landscape provides clear evidence why these are called the Rocky Mountains. Everywhere are rocks: piled rocks, or cairns, carefully placed to mark the path by those who have gone before; steps and stairs made of rocks; benches of rock that sit next to granite boulders the size of homes. Atop it all is a smooth slide of nearly vertical rock as long as a city block, carrying a stream of water from the melting snow above.

This rocky place offers dramatic views of the valley and the sparkling lakes below and provides a perfect resting spot to view the towering spectacle of Lone Peak above. It's as if Mother Nature is subtly teaching that you can't look down and look up at the same time.

Gazing upward at the fortress of rock, I realize that the giant steel-and-glass skyscrapers of New York and Hong

Kong have nothing on the sixty-story spires of stone that stretch into the clouds as they scrape the sky.

Upon the tallest of these natural towers nature has painted with water-leached minerals a distinctly visible question mark that is so large you can't quite believe what your eyes are seeing. Resting at an elevation of over 11,000 feet, it stands more than ten stories tall and is known to experienced climbers and hikers alike as Question Mark Wall.

The purpose of Question Mark Wall seems self-evident—a reminder that no matter how high we climb, we each need to reflect and ask: How did I get here? Have I been following the correct path? Am I on target? How do I overcome the obstacles ahead of me? Am I clear about where I really want to go? Do I recognize those who are waiting to help me on my path?

I leave my reverie and write in my journal that questions such as these, and their answers, have dominated my thoughts since I embarked on my own personal journey of discovering the secret power within words.

OPPORTUNITY MEETS DESTINY

It was in Vienna, after my new friend and guide Pravin Cherkoori appeared on my path and taught me *the* secret word, that, as fate would have it, I learned of another guide who would teach me that *all* words have secrets.

He was introduced to me by Bill Fillmore, an attorney who was part of our delegation that had traveled to Austria to meet with Viktor Frankl's family. Bill mentioned how he couldn't help but notice that I was constantly writing in my journal and wondered what I might be writing about.

"Words," I told him. "I'm learning all I can about words and the power within them."

I opened my journal and showed him the entry with the secret word that Pravin Cherkoori had taught me.

"Please, tell me more," Bill replied as his face broke into a grin as wide as the Cheshire cat's.

"I'm on a quest to uncover the secrets of words and what they meant originally when they first surfaced," I explained. "It's like peeling an onion. By breaking down words layer by layer, by uncovering their pure meaning, you tap into a force that will help you find your purpose and better lead your life."

Bill then revealed the reason for the big smile on his face.

"I want you to meet a mentor of mine," he said. "He knows more about words than any living human being I know."

The man's name, he said, is Arthur Watkins, a retired university professor who has devoted his lifetime to etymology, the study of words. He earned his PhD in linguistics from Stanford and spent nearly forty years teaching language at the university level. He is also fluent in a dozen languages. During World War II he helped decode German army transcriptions on the Italian front.

"And do you know what he does for fun?" Bill asked. "He loves to teach others about the origins of words. That is his favorite thing to do in all the world."

Bill explained that Arthur was now living in a

retirement home. "He is the undisputed Master of Words," he exclaimed. "You have to meet him."

Within days after returning from Vienna, I called Arthur.

While waiting for the phone to ring, I pictured someone frail and ashen, on oxygen perhaps, hooked to an IV in bed waiting to share the last morsel of wisdom from his life.

But after only half a ring, that illusion was shattered when a clear, confident voice answered, "Watkins residence."

"Hi, I'm Kevin Hall," I said. "Bill Fillmore gave me your number and said he'd tell you I'd call."

"I've been expecting your call," Arthur answered in a formal tone but with obvious enthusiasm.

"I was hoping we could get together sometime," I said, prepared to set up an appointment for later that week.

"I'm available tonight," he said readily.

I looked at my watch. It was nearly 8:00 p.m.

"I could be there within half an hour," I said, with some hesitation. I didn't want to invade his sleep time or violate any retirement home curfews. But the voice on the other end of the phone was unfazed. "That will be fine" came the answer. "I will be most pleased to have your company."

When I rang the doorbell at Arthur's room, he opened the door wearing khakis and a sweatshirt with an American flag on the front. On his feet were black Converse All-Stars. The All-American professor was in. (As I would learn on return visits, he was always in.) This was not a young man. He hunched slightly. His face was lined and wrinkled. His ears were outsized, and each had a hearing aid attached. When he smiled, he took on a Yoda-like tranquility. Everything about his visage spoke of wisdom and experience.

We shook hands, and he ushered me in. He sat in a recliner, and I took a seat on the couch to his right. That turned out to be on the side of his faulty hearing aid, however, and he quickly moved over and sat next to me on the couch. His knees and elbows nearly touched mine so he could better hear what I was saying. I immediately felt comfortable and surprisingly at ease. Although we were separated in age by over four decades, the connection between us was instant and, I sensed, mutually enthusiastic. My good friend, bestselling author Richard Paul Evans, is fond of sharing the Chinese aphorism "When the student is ready, the teacher will appear." I must have been ready, because appear he did.

It soon became obvious, as I looked around Arthur's twelve-by-twelve-foot room, that he loved words. The evidence was everywhere. On the coffee table was a dog-eared copy of a book Arthur proudly proclaimed to be his all-time favorite read: *Webster's New Collegiate Dictionary.* On one side of the couch was a thick, hardbound book, consisting of two volumes of his life's history. Each was single-spaced and double-columned. Combined they contained 1,416 pages and over one million words that Arthur claimed to be, in the matter-of-fact manner of the elderly that does not come off as boasting, "the longest, most complete autobiography ever written in either the modern or the ancient world." I asked to use his bathroom, and stuck smack dab in the middle of the mirror was his vocabulary word of the day. I marveled, *Here's a man in his ninth decade, at the very top of the language game, and every day he's learning a new word!*

That night I would discover that, as is the case in retirement homes everywhere, the wisdom, experience, and knowledge of those who live there truly knows no bounds. In Arthur's humble surroundings, I couldn't help but feel a bit overwhelmed.

"Kevin, tell me about yourself," Arthur said with a smile.

LEADERS FIND THE PATH

I told him about my family and interests and explained to him that for twenty-five years I had taught and developed leadership training. Along the way I had become fascinated by words and their power, I explained, and now I wanted to learn all I could about the secrets of words and how they might help us lead purpose-filled lives.

"It sounds like you're interested in leadership, in helping others lead their lives," he said. "Let's start our word study by examining the origin of the word 'leader.'"

He explained that the word is Indo-European, and that it is derived from two words. The first part—"lea"—means *path,* and the second part—"der"—means *finder.*

"A leader is a pathfinder," he said. "Leaders find the path. They are the readers of the signs and the clues. They see and show the way."

He paused, then continued. "Kevin," he said, "can you

imagine a hunting party going out in ancient days?" he asked, waving his arms and hands for dramatic effect. "Those who become the leaders see the sign of the game and stop to listen. They pause to catch their breath and get on their hands and knees to recognize the clues. They see the hoof marks. They are the ones with the best hearing who put their ears to the ground and listen to where the game is. They are the ones who touch the ground and can tell which direction the animal is traveling. In olden times, finding the true path of the game was life sustaining.

"Being a leader means finding the path," he continued, then added, "but before you can help someone else find their path, you must know yours."

What he said gave me a whole new picture, a word picture, of what it means to be a leader. Arthur had opened my eyes to see words in a dimension I never dreamed of. If it's true that a picture is worth a thousand words, it's also true that a word is worth a thousand pictures.

In one short visit my new teacher revealed that words, all words, have an essence, and by understanding that essence, we are in a position to be able to use them to light our paths.

I spent over two hours with Arthur that first night. We studied more than a dozen words, but it felt as if minutes had passed. When I looked at my watch and saw it was 10:30, I could scarcely believe it.

As I walked to the parking lot, I felt a chill run up and down my spine, a repeat of the feeling I had experienced just days earlier in Vienna when I met Pravin. First, my path led me to a guide waiting to teach me about a very powerful word. Tonight, halfway around the world in a retirement home no more than thirty minutes from my front porch, my path led me to a teacher waiting to instruct me about the power of all words.

Again, Pravin's parting words to me rang loud, clear, and true. It is a journey. We are all on a journey. And when we follow our path, we find those who show us the way. It is not just some mystical, abstract concept, a metaphor, a figure of speech, a mathematical impossibility. It can be, and usually is, a very real, very physical experience.

LIFE ISN'T PRACTICE

A few years ago, I was scoutmaster of a Boy Scout troop and we were in the Grand Tetons in northwestern Wyoming for our summer camp. There were eighteen of us, including leaders. On the morning the boys were to attempt to pass the toughest requirement for their hiking merit badge, the dreaded twenty-mile hike, I gathered them around the campfire to talk about the importance of setting goals to give you direction and focus in your life. Peter Vidmar, a two-time gold medalist in the Olympics in gymnastics and one of the country's top speakers, had recently told me about appearing at a conference with one of the world's most respected human behavioralists, Dr. Gerald Bell, a professor at the University of North Carolina in Chapel Hill. Peter told me about a survey Dr. Bell had recently completed that studied the lives of 4,000 retired executives. He had spoken to these proven business leaders, whose average age was seventy, in their homes, in senior centers, and in rehabilitation hospitals, and he'd asked them just one question: *If you could live your life over again, what would you do differently?*

To build up Dr. Bell's credibility with the Scouts, I told them how he had helped the North Carolina basketball team win the national championship when a freshman named Michael Jordan was on the team. Before the season started, Dr. Bell and Coach Dean Smith had gone to every player's locker and hung a poster of the Louisiana Superdome, site of that year's national championship game. The idea was to get every player to visualize playing in that game in that arena. The poster served as a positive visual image that was worthy of their highest commitment. Every day before practice, and again after practice, the players would open their lockers, and there, staring back at them, was a reminder of what they were aiming to achieve. It was an image that said: *You can do this. Focus on this. You are worthy of this. It will be worth it!* For the entire season they could see their goal. They could almost hear the cheering when they closed their lockers. And at the end of the season they achieved what they had envisioned. They played their final game in the Louisiana Superdome, Michael Jordan made the game-winning shot, and they won the national championship.

After that remarkable year, Dr. Bell and Dean Smith co-wrote the *New York Times* bestseller *The Carolina Way.* Dean Smith, I explained to the Scouts, was the coach of Michael Jordan's physical skills. Dr. Gerald Bell was his mind coach.

As these twelve- to fourteen-year-old Scouts looked up

at me, I told them what those seventy-year-old executives answered when Dr. Bell asked them what they would do differently if they could live their lives over again.

Their top response, an answer that ranked far ahead of any others, was this: *I should have taken charge of my life and set my goals earlier. Life isn't practice, it's the real thing.*

I shared the rest of the survey answers with the Scouts: (2) *I would have taken better care of my health.* (3) *I would have managed my money better.* (4) *I would have spent more time with my family.* (5) *I would have spent more time on personal development.* (6) *I would have had more fun.* (7) *I would have planned my career better.* (8) *I would have given more back.*

The young, impressionable faces around the fire displayed varying degrees of attention. My goal was that they would start thinking about their future, and of more urgency, what they could do that very day. What were their real goals for today's hike? What was their sense of commitment? Were they determined to make it? Would they be content with just finishing the bare requirements, or did they want to set their sights higher?

Later on during the hike, some of the Scouts started to lag, and I challenged them to go beyond the required twenty miles that finished at String Lake, and go a half mile farther to Bearpaw Lake. If they'd do that and return to String Lake, they'd hike twenty-one miles. I promised anyone who went the extra distance that I'd take them into Jackson Hole and buy them the best steak dinner of their life at the Million Dollar Cowboy Steakhouse. They would see that there was a reward for going the extra mile.

I had four takers out of fifteen Scouts. We left the rest of the pack behind and started jogging away, eager about the prospects of going beyond what was required. But several miles later, as we reached the turnoff where you could take the quick and easy trail to String Lake or persevere along the more challenging route to Bearpaw Lake, two of the Scouts had a change of heart. It was interesting that these were boys who had never had to deal with many hard challenges in their lives. Some could say that their lives had been so privileged that they were born on third base and thought they'd hit a triple. By the time we reached the crossroads, they were content with finishing the hike as quickly as possible. Instead of going on to Bearpaw Lake, they made a beeline for String Lake.

In contrast, the two Scouts who stayed were boys who were always up for a challenge, willing to go higher, to risk, grow, and expand their comfort zone. For boys who ranged from ages twelve to fourteen, it was impressive to watch. What kind of home life instilled this in them?

After reaching Bearpaw Lake and turning around, knowing we just needed the final, gradual downhill half mile to go to realize our stretch goal (and their steak dinner), I looked down the trail and saw a fit runner with a beautiful stride come into view. He was wearing glasses, looked to be in his midfifties, and instead of the painful look we see in many runners, was wearing a big smile. I was enthused by the sight of new company, for it is seldom crowded on the extra mile. When he was closer, he called out, "Are you Scoutmaster Kevin Hall?" I mentally joked to myself, *How can creditors find me here in the Grand Tetons?*

"Yes, I am," I responded.

"I just ran into two of your Scouts, and they're worried that you might get lost and not find your way back," he said. "Do you mind if I jog along with you and help show you the way?"

I laughed and said, "Thanks. I know the route, but we'd love the company." Then I asked him what brought him to the Tetons.

"I'm on vacation. I love this area of the country," he answered.

I asked where he was from.

"I'm from North Carolina."

"What part of North Carolina?"

"Chapel Hill."

To which I responded, "You wouldn't happen to know a Dr. Gerald Bell, would you?"

He stopped dead in his tracks, as did I, only to have the two Scouts behind us practically run right up our backs.

He looked at me incredulously and said, "Well . . . I . . . am . . . Dr. . . . Gerald Bell!"

I'm not sure who was more astonished by this chance meeting, but as we recovered from our amazement, we started again to jog while I explained to Dr. Bell how that very morning at our campfire devotional we had talked about his study of the 4,000 retired executives.

I asked him, "Is it true that the one thing they would do differently if they could live over again is carve out their life's goals earlier?"

"That is absolutely true," he said.

The two Scouts were stunned and delighted that our paths had literally crossed. I couldn't have been more pleased to talk to anyone in the universe right then and there than Dr. Bell, who continued to run along the trail beside us, providing additional insights and details about his study and enthusiastically stressing the importance of taking charge of your life through goal setting. Those Scouts learned a great lesson: when you go the extra mile, amazing things happen.

As we parted, I asked Dr. Bell what he thought the chances were of our meeting on the trail on the very day I shared his study with the Scouts. He said he couldn't put a number on it, maybe one in a trillion. Or, as one of the Scouts put it, "one in infinity."

But it did happen, and it does happen. As Joseph Campbell taught so vividly in *The Power of Myth,* "When you follow your bliss, you put yourself on the track that has been there all the while . . . you begin to meet people who are in the field of your bliss, and they open doors to you."

While some might choose to attribute it to coincidence, or happenstance, or simply dumb luck, I know that when we aspire to achieve our goals, each connection that we make leads to another and another and another.

Keys to Pathfinding

In devoting a significant part of my life to the study of human potential and development, I have come to realize that those who follow their true path and purpose do five things: (1) they are able to read the clues that guide them on their path; (2) they are very clear about where they are going; (3) they recognize and embrace their natural gifts; (4) they are willing to sacrifice to make significant contributions; and (5) they follow their bliss, and as a result they meet people on their path who have been placed there to guide them along their journey.

"And when I think about it," Paulo Coelho writes in the final line of *The Pilgrimage,* "I guess it is true that people always arrive at the right moment at the place where someone awaits them."

My Journal Thoughts on *Pathfinder*

Carrying two books is crucial to discovering my path. As the great adventure writer Robert Louis Stevenson said, "All through my boyhood and youth ... I kept always two books in my pocket, one to read, one to write in."

I have a unique path, and the book I write in is the map of that special path. It's a record of my own heroic journey. It's where I've been and where I'm going.

In Old French, "journée" meant a day's travel. My journal is a record of the clues that I discover on my path each day. "Journal" means a day. I will write in and review my journal on a daily basis.

By setting aside regular reflection time, I find joy in the journey. I will take just one percent of each day—approximately fifteen minutes—and use it to reflect on the past twenty-four hours and contemplate on the possibilities that lie ahead.

Four things I need to recognize daily:
1. People who appear on my Path to help me fulfill my Purpose.
2. Actions taken on Opportunities.

3. Thoughts that help me create a life of Meaning and Significance.

4. Moments of Happiness and Bliss.

People. Actions. Thoughts. Happiness.
That spells PATH!

This written witness of my journey helps me stay on my PATH and travel in the direction of my PURPOSE.

IDENTIFY AND HONOR A
Pathfinder

SELECT someone you know whose behavior best reflects a true Pathfinder.

WRITE that person's name in the box provided below.

REACH OUT to and teach that person the meaning of "Pathfinder" and explain why he or she personifies this word.

CHAPTER THREE

❧

Namasté

To be nobody but yourself in a world
which is doing its best, night and day,
to make you everybody else—means to fight the
hardest battle which any human being can fight.

— **E. E. CUMMINGS** —

There is a path along the California coast that I love to walk. Its course mimics the shoreline as it meanders a stone's throw from the sandy beach and the pulse of the Pacific Ocean just beyond. The sun is warm, the breeze consistent; the smell, seasoned with salt, is delicious. On the sand, people sit in beach chairs reading, or sunbathe, or jog to the point and back, while children build castles and surfers catch waves, and on the horizon ships ply the waters bound for distant lands. In a place that tends to attract only those who want to be there, the mood is tranquil, and it is reflected in the friendly greetings. When I smile and say hello to someone on that path, I can count on getting a smile and hello in return.

I have often wondered what reaction I would get if, instead of "Hi" or "Hello" or "How are you doing?" I said, "Namasté."

I have never actually done this, mainly because I can see my family recoiling in horror, but if ever there was a word that ought to be exported from East to West, it is this sacred greeting that translates as "I salute the Divine within you; I salute your God-given gifts."

It is appropriate that a greeting that shows such respect

has a unique and reverential way of being expressed. Before "Namasté" (pronounced nah-mah-STAY) is spoken, the palms of the hands are pressed together, the head is bowed, and the hands touch the heart. Devotees of yoga, where Namasté is commonly expressed, will recognize the movement.

Albert Einstein learned of the word "Namasté" and its meaning after watching Mahatma Gandhi in a newsreel greeting people in the streets of India by bowing with his hands pressed together. Einstein wrote Gandhi and asked what he was saying.

Gandhi replied: "Namasté. It means I honor the place in you where the entire universe resides. I honor the place in you of light, love, truth, peace, and wisdom."

Imagine what impact this single word could have on the world if every day you looked each person that you passed in the eye and said, in effect:

I salute the Divine within you. I salute what you do best. I salute your natural gifts. I honor your uniqueness and your specialness.

EVERY PERSON IS AN UNREPEATABLE MIRACLE

The symbolism of Namasté carries a message of peace and harmony and salutes the connectivity and divinity of all beings. Namasté sends a clear signal that I am not armed and mean you no harm—much like the Western handshake, which originated out of warfare as a clear way of demonstrating that you are not carrying any weapons.

But Namasté is so much more than a symbol of peace. It recognizes that no one, not one soul, in the human family is exempt from receiving gifts that are uniquely his or her own. No matter how alike we might appear, based on our race, ideology, where we live, what political party we belong to, or how we wear our hair—if we have hair—each of us is truly one of a kind. Over six billion people are on the earth, yet not one of us has the same fingerprints, or footprints, or even laugh. Every individual is authentic. Every person is an unrepeatable miracle.

In a cookie-cutter world where conformity is routinely demanded, it is easy to lose sight of the fact that we are each unique. How many times do we communicate to our children, to our spouse, to our employees, "Why can't you be more like (fill in the blank)?" How often are business managers, salespeople, educators, teenagers, athletes, and hundreds of others told that there is one way, and only one way, to act or to perform a certain task?

How often do we fail to recognize how unique we truly are? And how often do we squelch our natural gifts and growth in the process—when these are the very things that would make our contribution more valuable?

DARE TO ASPIRE

When I was nineteen years old, a friend gave me a copy of a classic book entitled *I Dare You!* It was the first self-improvement book I ever read. It was originally published in 1931 in the throes of the Great Depression, and was written by a man named William Danforth, founder of the Ralston Purina Company and co-founder of the American Youth Foundation.

The book was in its twenty-sixth printing by the time

I read it. It had survived the Depression and then some. In its pages, Danforth dares you to be your authentic best self, motivating each of us—if we accept the dare—to aspire to aim higher.

The middle chapter, "I Dare You to Build Character," relates a story I will never forget. "There is a Hindu legend," Danforth recounts,

> that at one time all men on earth were gods, but that men so sinned and abused the Divine that Brahma, the god of all gods, decided that the godhead should be taken away from man and hid some place where he would never again find it to abuse it. "We will bury it deep in the earth," said the other gods. "No," said Brahma, "because man will dig down in the earth and find it." "Then we will sink it in the deepest ocean," they said. "No," said Brahma, "because man will learn to dive and find it there, too." "We will hide it on the highest mountain," they said. "No," said Brahma, "because man will some day climb every mountain on the earth and again capture the godhead." "Then we do not know where to hide it where he cannot find it," said the lesser gods. "I will tell you," said Brahma. "Hide it down in man himself. He will never think to look there." And that is what they did. Hidden down in every man is some of the Divine. Ever since then he has gone over the earth digging, diving and climbing, looking for that godlike quality which all the time is hidden down within himself.

In her book *A Return to Love,* bestselling author Marianne Williamson writes eloquently about the instinct within us that recognizes our God-given gifts: "Our deepest fear is not that we are inadequate. Our deepest fear is that we are powerful beyond measure."

At our essence, at our core, in our quietest moments, as we move past that fear we can embrace the greatness that lies within.

Afternoons with Arthur

Arthur was a picture of enthusiasm when I walked into his room for our Thursday afternoon word study session at the Summerfield Manor retirement home. I had grown accustomed to his youthful exuberance. His hearing was going, he moved with a walker, there was plenty he couldn't eat, but his love for words and language was as intense as it had ever been.

As we discussed the meaning of Namasté, Arthur began to stomp his feet like an excited twelve-year-old. "Oh, Kevin, I love words! I just love words!" he exclaimed.

He loved words almost as much as he loved his wife, Ruth, who died in 2000. He loved to reminisce about her. Pictures of her, a beautiful woman with auburn hair, were spread around the room.

He told me about their honeymoon in 1941 and talked about the fun they had as they toured the national parks, although he confessed there was one uneasy moment when his new bride caught him in the closet, curled up with the Hebrew dictionary.

He was memorizing the Hebrew alphabet.

"You were memorizing the Hebrew alphabet on your honeymoon?" I asked with feigned disbelief. I knew by now that if Arthur said it, he wasn't stretching the truth.

"Yes," he said, still acting boyishly sheepish about it sixty-six years later. He had cheated on his wife—with a book about language. He loved them both.

Words inspired emotion for Arthur. He delighted in telling me about the first time he heard German spoken and how it nearly brought him to tears as he listened to the poetic sounds and graceful simplicity of the language. He said he was unable to eat, or sleep, until he began to learn that beautiful language.

As we discussed the meaning of Namasté, Arthur observed, "That sounds like it comes from the same origin as our English word 'enthusiasm.' Originating with the Greeks, 'enthusiasm' means *God within* or *God's gifts within.*"

Enthusiasm, he went on to explain, is the fuel of happiness and bliss. It refers to the divine light that shines within each of us.

As the Master of Words talked, I looked around his room at the evidence of his unique gifts—a pile of lecture notes, a dog-eared dictionary, numerous books on etymology and word origins—and how he used them to fuel a lifetime of happiness and bliss.

Now that Arthur was warmed up, he started to branch out to a whole family of words that related to Namasté.

He introduced the word "authentic" and explained that it comes from two words. One is "autos," which means *self,* and the other is "hentes," which means *being.*

"Authentic," he smiled as he moved his hands for effect, "means *being yourself."*

Namasté salutes authenticity. Society often does not.

He also talked about the word "genius" and explained that it comes from the Roman "genuinus," which means *what you were naturally born with.* Genius is nothing more, or less, than being "genuine."

People who follow their nature develop their genius, taking it further and further with each new challenge, never being satisfied with today's comfort zone.

The discussion turned to the word "character," the meaning of which, Arthur explained, has changed significantly over the years. Originally, it meant something that was engraved—on wood, on metal, on stone, on one's soul. Character is who you are; it is you in totality—the composite of everything that has ever happened to you, all the good and all the bad experiences.

In Shakespeare's time, character acquired an alternate meaning—quite the opposite. It became the word that described a part that an actor played. Characters acted out roles, wearing masks to hide their true identity. Instead of defining who you were, character defined who you were not.

The world can and will hide our identity if we are not careful. Conformity, pigeonholing, focusing on flaws instead of greatness, conspires to disguise our God-given gifts, our Namasté, and distract and take us away from our true path and purpose. Instead of "To thine own self be true," we become a character playing a part prescribed by others. We futilely try to be all things to all people and satisfy no one.

I had a question for Arthur. "If we're supposed to salute the gifts within ourselves and others, how do we recognize what those gifts are?"

Arthur taught me the meaning of "recognize," and it was for me like learning it for the first time.

"Re" is *again,* and "cognize" is a derivative of "cognizant," which means *to know.* Recognize means *to know again.*

Recognizing your natural gifts is like meeting an old friend. It feels like coming home. And you *are* coming home; you are coming home to your authentic, genuine self. The feeling is blissful, natural, and unmistakable.

You will know because it will flow.

By tapping into his natural gifts, his love of words, Arthur has been able to seamlessly knit together his vocation with his avocation. As is often the case with those who honor their Namasté, his play became his work, and his work became his play.

A TALENT WASTED IS A SIN

I was a season ticket holder of the Utah Jazz the year they qualified to play the Chicago Bulls for the NBA championship. My wife, Sherry, and I were fortunate to be in Houston for the Western Conference championship game when the Jazz earned their first-ever trip to the NBA Finals when John Stockton hit "The Shot" over Charles Barkley. The next morning we flew home and had just stepped in our front door and were hugging the kids when my daughter handed me the telephone. She said it was somebody from Chicago calling for me.

The voice on the other end said, "Hi, this is Gene Siskel." Well, it didn't register with me who Gene Siskel was. I said, "Excuse me, could you repeat your name?" and his voice rose slightly as he said, "You know, Gene Siskel of *Siskel and Ebert and the Movies.*"

Finally, I made the connection that I was talking to the *Chicago Tribune* movie reviewer—the man who invented "two thumbs up."

He explained that he was calling because he'd heard that I had tickets in the Jazz arena directly behind the visiting team's bench, a bench that would be occupied during the upcoming series by his favorite basketball team in the whole world, the Chicago Bulls. He wanted to trade two front-row tickets in the United Center in Chicago for my four tickets at the Delta Center in Utah. We laughed and joked as I explained the math that four didn't quite equal two. But eventually we came up with a trade that made us both happy and began a friendship that lasted until Gene was sadly taken from us far too early by a malignant brain tumor.

When we flew to Chicago for the games there, Gene and his wife, Marlene, took Sherry and me to Gibson's, "the finest steak house in the city." As Gene and I talked about life's twists and turns, we soon discovered we had much in common. Even though our tastes in basketball teams were night and day, our views on life were surprisingly similar.

Not long into our discussion, Gene made a statement I'd never heard before, and I've since never forgotten.

"Kevin," he said, "a talent wasted is a sin."

He continued, "We all have certain talents we've been given. I'm not just saying it's unused potential to not develop your talent, I'm saying it's a sin."

I began to realize why he felt so strongly about this subject when he told me about his childhood. He explained he lost his mother and father at an early age and was raised, along with a sister and brother, by an aunt and uncle who treated the Siskel children as their own. That special uncle taught him that talents are given to each of us for a reason, and it was his responsibility to develop his talent, expand it, and then do something useful with it.

"I realized at a fairly early age that I was very visual and auditory, and I just loved movies," Gene said. "That was my passion, that was what I was naturally attracted to, and I always wanted to share that love of movies with others. Who knew you could make a living at it? But that's what I did, and that's what I do, and as far as I'm concerned, I've never worked a day in my life."

Gene described Namasté at its elemental level: before we can salute the greatness within others, we need to salute the greatness within ourselves.

IDENTIFYING OUR UNIQUE GIFTS

When I was just starting out in the human development field at Franklin, leading the sales team, Denis Waitley, author of *The Psychology of Winning*, recommended I spend two days at the Johnson O'Connor Research Foundation, also known in its early days as the Human Research Laboratory. There, they could test me to determine my natural gifts. As he explained, "They give you a series of tests, some of them physical, some of them mental. When it's over, they assess what you have a natural affinity for and what you don't." I accepted Denis's advice and wound up taking my test next to a nun. She must have wanted to be the best she could be, bar none.

The test is a thorough assessment of a person's natural gifts. In some areas I didn't score that well. For instance, there is a category called "tweezer dexterity" that tests how well you work with your fingers and your hands. I was awful at that. If I'm your brain surgeon, you're going to die. The nun just killed me in tweezer dexterity. The test results also strongly suggested that I shouldn't become a structural engineer.

But the emphasis, rather than negative, is positive. The idea isn't to expose a person's weaknesses; it's to identify that individual's strengths. After dashing any hopes I might have had to be a neurosurgeon, build bridges, or design great buildings, the testers said to me, "Do you know where you are off the charts? Do you know what you are naturally good at? Do you know where you place in the top five percent of the hundreds of thousands we have tested over the years?"

They had my attention.

"You have a profound strength for ideaphoria," they told me. "That is your strongest gift."

To be honest, I had never heard the term "ideaphoria" before. The test that identified this unrecognized strength was simple. The testers placed a single word in front of me and handed me a blank piece of paper. Then they instructed me to write all my thoughts about that word as they timed me. When my time was up, I had filled both sides of the piece of paper and had run out of room, yet I felt as though I hadn't finished. One word was all it took to get my mind racing.

Ideas! That was my gift. I could be great at that!

To be true to myself, to really shine, I need to create, explore, write, and constantly search for what is just beyond the edge. "You were meant to create and market," my Johnson O'Connor analyst advised me, "but not in an atmosphere where you have to conform to someone else's strategies and plans. You need to find a way to be free to explore your own creative innovations and ideas. You need to do that to follow your path and manifest your gifts and talents." And if I didn't do that, I would be guilty of what my friend Gene Siskel called a sin.

What I learned at Johnson O'Connor was not really a surprise. Deep down I knew what my gifts were and had known it intuitively all my life. The testers confirmed what I already was aware of. Sometimes I get a flood of ideas that come so quickly and with so much force that I don't dare eat, or shower, or even go to the bathroom for hours. That is why I always carry my journal on my path, so I can instantly write them down. As I learned in Napoleon Hill's *Think and Grow Rich,* "The best time to nurse an idea is at the time of its birth. Every minute it lives gives it a better chance of surviving." When ideas come, you can use them or lose them; you can put them down on paper or risk letting them fly away.

I have since identified my personal statement of purpose, which is to connect words, ideas, and people. My passion is helping others connect to their path and fulfill their purpose in life. When I am connecting two people together, I feel as if I'm filling both sides of that sheet of paper. I see untold numbers of ways two people can contribute to each other's needs and successes.

What Do You Know for Sure?

Gene Siskel had a signature line. He would say, "What do you know for sure?" It was actually as much a reminder as a question: are we focusing on what we love, on what comes naturally, on what we do best? That thought—*What do you know for sure?*—can be found on the last page of every issue of Oprah Winfrey's *O* magazine. Oprah credits Gene for the insightful line, and by printing it at the end of each magazine, she reinforces the importance of that simple yet profound question.

In my estimation, "What do you know for sure?" is the essence of the Johnson O'Connor natural gifts assessment. The evaluation was invaluable to me, a wake-up call to focus on what I do best. Recognizing that is paramount. If we don't recognize our gifts, we can't use them. How can you appreciate a gift that you don't open?

People at the top of the learning curve, those who excel in their field, the crème de la crème, the best of the best, those who tend to shine just a little brighter, focus on one thing: their unique gifts. They often comment that they would do what they do for free.

BMW is a valued client of mine, and they asked me to come in and create a language that sells versus a language that repels. That assignment led me to the No. 1

BMW client advisor in North America, Neda Shahrokhi. Neda sells approximately nine hundred brand-spanking-new BMWs a year. You heard that right. Nine hundred. That's three a day, virtually every day of the year. And she has done it consistently from year to year whether the economy is good or bad. The secret to her extraordinary success, she told me, is that "I don't have any unique sales techniques. I don't manipulate someone into buying a car. I'm not a closer. But I am great at creating relationships. For me, selling a car is not about the close. A close is a short-term transaction. I'm gifted at creating meaningful relationships that are long term. Selling a car is simply providing a service for my friends. I would do what I do for free."

This is often the case with those who honor their Namasté. When you feel as if you would do something for free, *that* is when you know you are on your true path. That is when you know you are connecting to what comes naturally to you.

Alice Elliot, who is widely regarded as one of the most influential people in the vast hospitality industry, recently told me that she used to make up her own business cards as a child. She said, "I always knew I would be in business. I used to sit on my bed and draw my name and my title on small pieces of paper: 'Alice Elliot, President and CEO.' I would hand these cards out to all of my friends."

Now Alice is president and CEO of the Elliot Group, a highly respected executive search firm, and hands out her cards to CEOs and executives throughout her industry.

Follow Your Nature

It's been said that nature works, but nature doesn't work. The evidence surrounds us. Everything about Mother Nature is harmony and flow. She doesn't fight the elements, she embraces them. Rivers don't try to run uphill. Plants don't try to grow in the Arctic. Animals thrive in their natural state.

The other day a beautiful red-tailed hawk, nature's perfect soaring machine, flew outside my window, floating in the air like a kite on a string. It took only an occasional flap of the wings to float there for what seemed like forever. It looked effortless. That hawk was free, free to be itself. It was doing what it was meant to do, doing what it does best.

In my training seminars, I frequently ask those in attendance what type of power they want most. Their No. 1 response, without fail, is to fly. They want to be free.

If you want to really fly in your life, if you want to soar higher than you ever thought humanly possible, then feel free to *be yourself*. Feel free to follow your nature.

We've all heard the expressions "You're a natural," "That's in your nature," "It's second nature to you," and "You were born to do that." "Nature" comes from the Latin "natura," which means *to be born* or *to give birth*. Nature is the gifts you were born with; it's your genius, the "genie within us." And that genie will grant your every worthwhile wish and dream.

Do What You Were Born to Do

The biggest mistake people make is not making a living doing what they love to do. Aren't parents' fondest wish and greatest desire that their children discover the potential that is within them? I'm not so concerned about the grades my children get, or the schools they attend, or the careers or businesses that they will launch. I don't care how much money they make, as long as they make enough to eventually move out of the house. What I want most for my children, and what I believe most parents want for their posterity, is to have them discover and recognize their Namasté and live it every day. If they do that, the rest of life—the grades, the job, the career, the money—will take care of itself.

I remember my daughter Season calling me from college. She was studying to become a teacher. When I answered the phone, I could feel the confusion in her voice. She said, "Dad, when I went in to finalize my classes, it just didn't feel right. I've always wanted to be a teacher. You and Mom always said I'd make a great teacher. You've encouraged me to be a teacher. But do you know what I really want to do? I want to design clothing. You know how I always make belts and purses, and when I wear them at work people ask me where I got them, and I tell them I made them, and then I eventually sell my designs to them? That's what I want to do." And I said, "Well, Season, why don't you do what you want to do?" At that point in her life she was in many ways unhappy. She was not on her path. She needed to start doing what was calling to her. She has since become a successful fashion designer. She has her own clothing line for children called Little Season. She has a style all her own. She's not trying to be the next Donna Karan, or the next Nicole Miller. She's the next Season Hall Everton.

In *The Power of Myth,* Joseph Campbell writes, "The way to find out about your happiness is to keep your mind on those moments when you feel most happy, when you really are happy—not excited, not just thrilled, but deeply happy. What is it that makes you happy? Stay with it no matter what people tell you. This is what I call following your bliss."

Your Unique Path

When you maximize your talents, you are on path, on purpose, on target. When you don't, you're off path, off purpose, off target.

Do you ever say to yourself, "I'm stressed . . . I'm overloaded . . . I'm going to have a breakdown"? We all feel like that occasionally, in small moments of our life, but if you are feeling that way consistently, regularly, from the moment you get up in the morning until the moment you go to bed, you're clearly not on your path, and you're most likely not doing what you were meant to do. Those three words—"stress," "overloaded," "breakdown"—were not originally meant to describe humans. They were meant to describe machines. They first surfaced during the Industrial Age. When the assembly line at the factory was stressed or overloaded, it eventually had a breakdown.

In one of his rare writings, the wise Sufi Hafiz teaches: "Because there are no formulas to attain the truth of the road, each of us must run the risk of his own steps. Only the ignorant seek to imitate the behavior of others. Intelligent men waste no time with that, they develop their personal abilities, they know there are no leaves alike in a forest of 100,000 trees. No two journeys on the same road are alike."

As you travel on your journey, remember that the footprints you leave on your path are as unique as the path you are walking.

Selecting Your Word

The first thing I do when I'm coaching someone who aspires to stretch, grow, and go higher in life is to have that person select the one word that best describes him or her. Once a person does that, it's as if he or she has turned to a page in a book and highlighted one word. Instead of seeing three hundred different words on the page, the person's attention, and intention, is focused immediately on that single word, that single gift. What the individual focuses on expands.

You can do this yourself or ask your friends and family, the people who know you best, what one word they would use to describe you. The word might be "artist," "wordsmith," "communicator," "director," or "teacher." It could be "peacekeeper," "perfectionist," or "musician." Maybe it's "organizer," "manager," "connector," or "leader." There are no restrictions other than it must be only one word, and the ultimate decision is up to you.

When you arrive at your word, write it on your bathroom mirror, your rearview mirror, your inner mirror, your desk, your computer, your refrigerator, next to your car keys, anywhere that you will be sure to see it on a daily basis. It is your greeting of Namasté—a salute from your heart to the special gifts within you.

Can you imagine what kind of a magical life, what kind of an extraordinary world, you would live in if you greeted yourself each day in such a magical, respectful way? You will change your world. Look in the mirror again, look at your word, reflect on your gifts, and remember the wise counsel of Mahatma Gandhi: "You must be the change you wish to see in the world."

You will change the world.

Namasté.

My Journal Thoughts on *Namasté*

I was born with inimitable gifts and talents. I honor the Giver of those gifts by opening them and giving of them freely.

Talents and gifts do not reduce or diminish when shared; they expand and increase like the widening ripples from a pebble dropped in still water.

Nobel laureate Aleksandr Solzhenitsyn taught that "talent is always conscious of its own abundance and does not object to sharing."

Tapping into my natural gifts is the first and most important step toward living a life of abundance and fulfillment.

"Abundance" originated from the undulation and bounty of the sea. Each wave carries the anticipation of another succession of waves, attesting to the fact that nature gives all and loses nothing.

"Fulfillment" also comes from water. A vessel cannot overflow until it is first filled.

Discovering the intersection between what I feel in my heart and what the world needs helps me discover my mission and purpose in life.

I stay on path and purpose by recording in my journal those times when my heart's deep gladness is calling to me, when I'm experiencing joy and inner peace, when I'm overflowing with fulfillment and abundance.

Recognizing this pure feeling of happiness allows me to give freely of my gifts and salute the Divine within.

I commit to stop doing what I am <u>good</u> at and start doing what I am <u>great</u> at. That is Namasté at its very essence.

IDENTIFY AND HONOR A PRACTITIONER OF
Namasté

SELECT someone you know who honors their unique gifts.

WRITE that person's name in the box provided below.

REACH OUT to and teach that person the meaning of "Namasté" and explain why he or she personifies this word.

CHAPTER FOUR

Passion

This is the core of the human spirit . . .
If we can find something to live for—if we can
find some meaning to put at the center of our lives—
even the worst kind of suffering becomes bearable.

— VIKTOR FRANKL —

In the cold desert night Chad Hymas checked again to make sure all was right with his three-wheeled handbike. For the next eleven days and nights, he would be riding it in his attempt to set a world record for distance traveled on a bike by a quadriplegic.

Aided by the light of the trailing support vehicle's headlights, he glanced up at me on my bicycle with a look of nervousness and eagerness. He was understandably anxious about the dark highway ahead, yet ready to launch out. I was there to ride with him and to offer moral support for the first stretch of his journey.

Knowing it would be chilly and that Chad couldn't risk catching a cold, I brought enough warm clothing to cover him from head to toe. I insisted that he insulate himself with protective cover. He bundled up like a mummy and hit the road spiffed out in full winter cycling garb: thermal shoe covers, leg and arm warmers, a Windbreaker, full-fingered gloves, winter riding cap, and Oakley frames with clear lenses.

I smiled at the thought of the double take passersby might experience as they glanced our way and witnessed two seemingly mature adults on a desolate wasteland road chasing their shadows at midnight with blinking reflectors on their backs; one in particular, pursuing a grown-up dream dressed like a child in winter, riding what appeared to be a tricycle in the middle of July.

Not able to regulate his body temperature, Chad chose July to pursue his goal that so many said was impossible. He would ride through the desert in the day, cooling off with cold towels when he got hot, and ride at night, layering on clothing as the temperature dropped. His goal: to wheel day and night, stopping only when necessary for rest and sleep until he made it to Las Vegas—513 miles away.

Two years before, he lost the use of his legs and most of his upper body in a split-second accident while moving hay on his family's ranch. One minute he was lifting a one-ton bale of hay with his tractor, and the next moment that massive bale lurched backward off the fork and catapulted on top of his neck, pinning him to the tractor's steering wheel. He was rushed to the hospital, where skilled physicians saved his life but not his mobility. A severed spinal cord rendered him a quadriplegic. Except for limited use of his forearms, he was immobilized from the neck down.

Chad's life and his plans for it were forever altered. But even though his body was paralyzed, his ability to dream was not.

After the stay at the hospital and a short *Why me?* period that followed, Chad awakened to the reality that his life would go on. His wife, Shondell, and their two boys loved and needed him as much as ever. His role was not diminished in their eyes. If he couldn't physically work the family ranch anymore, he decided he needed to find new fulfillment and amended dreams for his radically altered body.

It was at this juncture that our paths crossed. A friend of a friend told him I had some experience in public speaking and arranged a meeting with Chad at my home. He told me he thought he had a story, and since, he joked, he could talk as well as he ever had, he was considering public speaking as a way to provide for his family.

The idea for the epic handbike marathon evolved from there.

If he was to deliver a message that would encourage and inspire others to follow their dreams, no matter what life brought, he wanted to have something tangible, some kind of physical evidence that would give him credibility that he had what it takes to conquer adversity.

The more dramatic, demanding, and memorable, the better, he figured. He was confident rolling 513 miles in a three-wheeled bike ("Never call it a tricycle," Chad would chide) powered by hands and arms with limited ability, from Salt Lake City to Las Vegas, in the sultry heat of summer would qualify on all three counts.

He had the desire, the incentive, and the support. Now, as he pedaled into the cold night, he would find out if he had what it really took. He would now discover if he had the passion.

PAYING THE PRICE

He wouldn't discover the depth of his passion at the starting line. We seldom do. When we set out on a quest, no matter how daunting or challenging, is there anything easier than the beginning?

When Chad pushed away from the starting line that sunny morning in July, it was all so easy. The police escort took him through red lights. Dozens of friends and family lined the streets, offering cheers and words of encouragement. His two young sons, Christian and Kyler, rode alongside on bicycles with beaming smiles. Total strangers applauded as he passed, wishing him well. The media were there, with television cameras rolling. He was the celebrity of the day. He would be on all the newscasts that night.

It wouldn't be until later, when the TV lights and police escorts were long gone, when there was no one on the curb to applaud and encourage, when the road turned upward, when his arms ached, when he was tired and hungry, that it would get difficult.

I rode with Chad for three days. Our relationship had turned into a friendship, and I was pulling hard for him to achieve the audacious goal he had set for himself.

The price his dream would exact became clear one particularly tough day as he faced a taxing eight-mile uphill climb. The heat was oppressive, radiating in waves from the asphalt well above one hundred degrees Fahrenheit at road level. Chad's body was positioned just four inches from the blistering pavement. With every turn of his crank I sympathized with the difficulty of the task ahead. Chad was struggling increasingly with the passing of every excruciating mile. The wind was in his face, the solitude increased with every curve, and the miles that had passed so quickly on the first day now agonizingly dragged on.

To make matters worse, a horde of crickets decided to use the same remote highway we were traveling. In seconds, thousands of the hopping creatures covered the pavement. On my bicycle I could see them hopping at my feet. But Chad, hugging the road, had it much worse as they swarmed over and under his extended legs and in and out of his seat and clothing. The sickening sight and sound of these leaping, chirping invaders intensified as our wheels couldn't help crushing the masses that got in the way. The repulsive stench of squashed invertebrates turned our stomachs, as did the ensuing scene of crickets cannibalizing the carcasses of their dead.

In the midst of this awful happening I recalled Chad's initial wishes for his marathon ride: *dramatic . . . demanding . . . memorable. Enough already,* I thought. *Mission accomplished.*

Just when it seemed time to turn around and leave this madness, two cars pulled up. As if on cue, two doors swung wide, and out popped two men on handbikes: one, a double-legged amputee; the other, a paraplegic with strapping arms and shoulders. They had seen the news on television the night before, and understanding what it was like to be in Chad's shoes, and chair, they decided he could use a little help and support. With full use of their powerful arms, they wheeled up and down the road like soldiers in a reconnaissance patrol, relaying critical information about the enemy and terrain ahead.

When it came time for me to leave Chad, I did so reluctantly. I could sense he was starting to have second thoughts. Later that night, as he rested in a motel room far from where he started and farther yet from where he wanted to end, he called me on the phone and wondered aloud what he was thinking when he dreamed up this crazy idea. It was just too hard, he told me. The degree of difficulty was crushing him. He wasn't sure if he could continue.

I responded as any friend would. I encouraged Chad to not give up, to not quit. I told him I knew he had what it took. After all, wasn't he the guy who already defied the odds and persevered for days, weeks, and months to learn again how to eat, how to brush his teeth, how to get dressed, how to sit up? I reminded him that he'd actually been training for this epic marathon for over a year and a half.

Then I hung up the phone and felt that helpless feeling we all get when we realize that people we care about have to make it on their own. As much as we would like to do it for them, it is up to them to decide if they are willing to suffer for what they want most.

Later, I would learn from the Master of Words that this process is summed up in a single word: "passion."

Afternoons with Arthur

It was Thursday afternoon, and I found myself eagerly waiting for Arthur's popular "Culture Capsule" lecture to begin. Every Thursday at 2:00 p.m. sharp, a handful of Arthur's fellow senior travelers at Summerfield Manor make their way to the living room just off the main entry in their walkers and wheelchairs, and through the power of words, Arthur, ever the professor, takes them on a linguistic journey around the world. As the handful of "regulars" trickle in, Professor Watkins presents them each with meticulously prepared lecture notes, printed in an incredibly tiny script I can't imagine cataract-challenged seniors being able to read.

Arthur addresses the intimate group of six as if he were speaking to a class of two hundred, with clear, precise pronunciation and professor-like diction, each word delivered with a fervent voice and an infectious first-day-of-class enthusiasm. Minutes into Arthur's oration, an elegantly dressed woman dozes off, triggering a domino effect of an involuntary jerking neck, flailing of arms and hands, and scattering of notes. The slumbering octogenarian awakens with a sheepish grin and reaches to retrieve her stray notes.

Arthur pays little attention to the distraction, focused on imparting his life's work to all those within the sound of his resonant voice. His lecture today is entitled "Growing Your Vocabulary from 800 Words to 600,000 Words." As the lesson progresses, Arthur moves from learning about words to learning from words. "By knowing the true meanings of words," he says, "we allow them to have a profound influence on our lives."

After the lecture we go down the hall to his room for what he referred to as our "word study."

The word I request we discuss today is "passion."

The Master of Words smiled and began, "The word 'passion' first surfaced in the twelfth century. Coined by

Christian scholars, it means *to suffer*. In its purest sense it describes the *willing suffering of Christ*."

After educating me about the word's etymology, Arthur added, "Passion doesn't mean just suffering for suffering's sake; it must be pure and willing suffering."

He continued, "I have attended many festivals and plays in Europe that commemorate Christ's suffering. They are called Passion plays."

Arthur said that both "passion" and "path" have similar roots: the word "path" is a suffix that means *suffering from*.

"Think about it, Kevin," said Arthur. "We have doctors called pathologists. They study the illnesses and diseases that humans suffer."

Then he revealed a link between suffering, or passion, and sacrifice. "The word 'sacrifice' comes from the Latin 'sacra,' which means *sacred,* and 'fice,' which means *to perform*. To sacrifice is *to perform the sacred*."

"At its essence," he continued, "'passion' is *sacred suffering*."

What Arthur uncovered penetrated deep inside my soul. Suffering isn't necessarily a bad thing. It can and should be a good thing. It's noble. It's sacred. It's life defining.

It's one thing to suffer and be a victim; it's an entirely different thing to be willing to suffer for a cause and become a victor.

Even though it has become popular to define passion as deep or romantic love, the real meaning is *being willing to suffer for what you love*. When we discover what we are willing to pay a price for, we discover our life's mission and purpose.

WILLINGNESS TO SUFFER

Passion is what sent Viktor Frankl into the hell of the Holocaust. As an esteemed surgeon, psychotherapist, and author, he could see what was happening. It was clear the Nazis would take over his beloved Vienna. He could have left, but he chose to stay because of his deep love for his parents, who could not obtain visas for themselves.

Elly Frankl, Viktor's second wife, shared the story with a group of us gathered on the outskirts of Vienna in a restaurant that was once the home of Ludwig van Beethoven. It was in this very home that Beethoven composed his greatest masterpiece, the Ninth Symphony, while completely deaf. Beethoven's final words were ever fitting: "I shall hear in heaven." He, too, had learned to elegantly master his suffering.

Elly told us how Viktor had arrived home from the American consulate with his travel visa in hand to find a large block of marble sitting on the table. His father had rescued it from a local synagogue that had been destroyed by the Nazis. It was, she recalled, a piece from a tablet bearing a commandment that read: "Honor thy Father and thy Mother, that thy days may be long upon the land."

Viktor put his travel visa in his drawer and never used it. He willingly chose to stay and suffer alongside his parents. He was at his father's side in the concentration camps and was able to administer medication that helped relieve his pain and suffering until his father died in his arms.

After the war was over, Viktor kept two prized pieces of art in his writing studio in Vienna. The first was a wooden carving of a man with an outstretched hand. The name of the piece: *The Suffering Man.* The second was a painting of ten coffins in Auschwitz. It was in one of these coffins that he found the remains of his father. They remain vivid reminders of why he went where he went and did what he did.

Passion stretches you. The sacred stretches you. Viktor's willingness to suffer led him to his gift. It led him to what he was meant to do—help others find meaning and purpose in life.

Viktor taught, "Our core drive as humans is our search for meaning. . . . The way in which a man accepts his fate, and all the suffering that it entails, the way in which he takes up his cross, gives him ample opportunity—even under the most difficult circumstances—to add a deeper meaning to his life."

We often find that meaning through suffering. Ralph Waldo Emerson said, "Every wall has a door." Passion in its purest sense, the willingness to suffer for what we love, is often the door that leads us to our path.

DISCOVERING COMPASSION

When I worked at Franklin, I loved to commute to the office on my bicycle, an hour each way. The fresh air and the physical exercise helped clear my mind so I was ready to create and engage the moment I stepped in the office door. But the riding would also tax me physically, and to help with that I paid regular visits to a massage therapist named Den Brinkley. Den had a reputation as a first-rate masseur. Not only did he get the knots out of my legs, he had a way of conversing that would get the knots out of my head.

One day I was biking and ran into someone. To be accurate, I should say he ran into me. I was traveling on my bike at about twenty miles an hour when the inebriated adolescent driver, fueled by methamphetamines and a six-pack of beer, hit me from behind going over sixty miles an hour. He had weaved into oncoming traffic attempting to pass a truck and narrowly avoided a head-on collision by swinging to the right, where he ran into me. It was a lethal combination: he was stoned, drunk, and never saw me. I bounced off the car's windshield and flew into the air, floating for what seemed an eternity until power line wires were at eye level. When I hit the pavement fifty-five feet later, everything started moving at warp speed. Like a rubber chicken, I flapped around until coming to a stop another sixty feet down the road. I looked back to see the car that hit me come to a screeching halt. I stared into the vacant eyes of the young man behind the steering wheel. He turned away, gunned his engine, and left me for dead.

An ambulance soon arrived and rushed me to the hospital. I hurt everywhere. I had whiplash, road rash, and a serious head injury. I was so nauseous I couldn't sit up. Miraculously, I was still alive. Dear friends brought my stunned wife to my bedside, then my oldest daughter arrived, and then came Den Brinkley, my masseur.

Den had to be the toughest guy I knew, the kind of man who can do a dozen one-arm pull-ups. On weekends he would fight wild boars and hogs with a knife; he was the ultimate warrior. If you were going to war, you would want to take him with you. In fact, Den had been to war, in Vietnam, where he was part of a reconnaissance patrol on the front lines. Den was the one person with the ability to get me out of that hospital. He understood my suffering. He knew what was going on with my body and the physical and psychological pain in my head.

He knew at a personal level how critical my situation was and how important it was for me to recover and said, "Kevin, did you know that at one time in my life I'd given up and was going to take my own life?"

Den said it had happened after he returned from Vietnam. He had seriously injured his back while working construction and was looking for another job when his wife said she didn't need him in her life, that nobody needed him in their life, and after cleaning out the bank account she took the good car and drove away, abandoning Den and their young son.

Early one evening, distraught and discouraged, he walked out behind his apartment with a loaded .45 and placed the barrel in his mouth.

He told me all this while he was massaging my body, attempting to bring me back to the living.

Then, just when he was seconds away from pulling the trigger, he heard a distant call, a call that became *his* summons back to the living—the call that gave him his purpose. "Daddy? Where are you, Daddy?" his son called out. "I *need* you. I can't find you. Daddy? Daddy? Where are you?"

"I put the gun down and wept like a baby because then and there I found something to live for," said Den. "My son saved my life that night."

And Den saved his son's life.

This reciprocal accountability of a father to a son, and a son to a father, was better expressed by Viktor Frankl: "A man who becomes conscious of the responsibility he bears toward a human being who affectionately waits for him, or to an unfinished work, will never be able to throw away his life. He knows the 'why' for his existence, and will be able to bear almost any 'how.'"

Den Brinkley knew I needed his gift. After hours of personal attention and rehabilitation that succeeded in getting me released from the hospital, he continued to come to my home each evening for the next several weeks. He would arrive after an eight- or nine-hour day of giving massages and then spend another hour or two massaging and manipulating my mangled body. Den demonstrated true compassion for me.

Compassion, I have come to learn, combines "com," or *with*, and "passion," or *suffer*. "Compassion" is to *suffer with another*. I will be forever grateful for how Den willingly suffered with, and for, me.

SUFFERING FOR WHAT MATTERS MOST

For a seven-letter word that originated well after most modern dictionaries were established, few words carry more strength and depth than "passion." Beyond prescribing what we need to do on a personal level to find purpose and meaning, it is also the word that best describes the heroic, selfless deeds done every day by one person for someone else. The list is a lengthy one: coaches, teachers, writers, mentors, trainers, therapists, psychologists, nurses, counselors, doctors—people who passionately and compassionately enrich and enlarge the lives of others.

And could there be a more consummate example of passion than a devoted mother?

Have you ever caught the eye of a mother in a crowded parking lot who has momentarily lost sight of her child? You would not want to get in the way of that passion. Mothers are willing to suffer for that child, that baby, that embryo in the womb. They endure nine months of suffering just to give birth, and their willingness to suffer for their children lasts a lifetime.

I watched my own mother sacrifice for my brother, Rick, and me. I watched my wife, Sherry, suffer to bring our six beautiful children into the world. And more recently I watched in awe as my oldest daughter, Summer, chose to give birth to a third child. This was not an easy decision because when she is pregnant, she is constantly nauseous, experiences severe migraine headaches, gets dizzy, and sees double, and she has to stay in bed a good deal of the time. Once I asked her, "Why would you put yourself through that?" She looked across the room at her two beautiful little girls. It didn't take a word, just that glance. That was why she willingly agreed to suffer again for nine long months.

All worthwhile contributions are achieved through passion, *if* one is willing to pay the price.

Anything Is Possible If You Are Willing to Pay the Price

One of my favorite and one of history's greatest self-improvement authors was once a down-and-out alcoholic who nearly spent his last few dollars on a suicide gun. He thought the world would be better off without him. Fortunately, for the countless millions whom his words have inspired, he turned from the cold beckoning of a handgun in a pawnshop window to the safe haven of a public library. That fortuitous shift in destination led him to a book with a message that would forever alter his life. The words inside the cover read, "You can accomplish anything you wish that is not contradictory to the laws of God or man, providing you are willing to pay a price." He knew then he had some unfinished work to complete.

Ever since he was a little boy he had dreamed of being a writer—a writer who could be of great service. That passage inspired him to now pursue that dream, and in so doing, he transformed himself from a despondent, unemployed salesman named Augustine, into Og Mandino, the gifted writer of the bestselling sales book of all-time, *The Greatest Salesman in the World*.

He summed it all up when he said, "How can you be unhappy or depressed when you know there's one person in the world who needs your gift, just one?"

Enduring to the End

As Chad rolled his handbike to the top of Apex Junction at four in the morning, he could see below him in the distance the glittering lights of Las Vegas, his ultimate destination. He told me later that just as no one could fathom the joy he felt at that moment, neither could they fathom the fatigue and despair he had faced during the hours and days prior to cresting that final hill. There were times, he said, when he was too tired to even weep. It had taken everything he had and then some. Chad had learned what Viktor Frankl meant when he said, "What is to give light must endure burning."

Chad had endured the burning of his neck when that massive bale of hay fell on him. He had endured the burning fear that overcame him in the dark hour when he came out of his surgery to discover that he would never walk again. He had endured the awful thought that he might not be able to take care of his family. He faced the fear that he might even lose them. Then he went on to relentlessly rehabilitate what was left of his body for eighteen long months.

And now, through a combination hell and heaven of his own making, he had endured the long, slow, all-important miles almost no one else sees or experiences. The middle of any journey always gets more difficult, as does the middle of accomplishing our highest aspirations and dreams.

That is where true passion comes in.

On our gravestone are two dates: the day we were born and the day we die. But what symbolizes our life is the dash in between. What happens in the middle? What happens between the traumatic moments? The euphoric moments?

In all those middle miles, when the temperature of the pavement soared above 120 degrees and his grip became so weak that his hands needed to be taped to his pedals and he was averaging less than two miles an hour, Chad went from counting hours to counting mile markers. When it got really tough, his father stepped in and said, "Son, instead of counting the green mile markers, why don't you count the yellow stripes in the middle of the road? They come a little faster. See if that helps." Chad was too numb to protest, and so he relearned something he already knew: by reducing that purpose to smaller and smaller steps, one day at a time, one mile at a time, one hour at a time, and even one yellow stripe at a time, your ultimate destination becomes achievable.

Just like at the beginning of the journey, it got easy again at the end. The police escort was back. Family and friends who had cheered at the start in Salt Lake City had flown to Las Vegas to cheer him at the finish. The media returned, the lights were on, the TV cameras were rolling. Strangers stopped in their tracks and applauded. All the intersection stoplights were turned off on the Las Vegas Strip as the Nevada Highway Patrol escorted Chad to the finish line in front of the Mirage Hotel. As he passed, people walked out of the casinos and applauded the man on the handbike who had pedaled 513 miles. There were no crickets.

Exhausted as he was at the finish, he didn't lose sight of his goals even then. Hearing of his accomplishment, an organization called and asked if he would be available to give a speech in three days—in Louisiana. Chad did not ask for time to recuperate. Immediately he started practicing his speech, got on a plane, and after previously receiving little more than gas money to talk to groups, he was paid handsomely.

He has since become a sought-after speaker. His clients include some of the biggest companies and organizations in the world. By the age of thirty-two, he became one of the youngest ever to earn the designation of certified speaking professional, a distinction given by the National Speakers Association to a select few. The *Wall Street Journal* called him "one of the ten most inspirational people in the world." He now generates a seven-figure income annually. But his greatest accomplishment is that he remains a devoted husband to his loving wife, Shondell, and a proud father to their three children, Christian, Kyler, and newly adopted Gracee.

Instead of letting outside influences determine the temperature and direction of his life, Chad chose to set his own controls and map out his own destiny. He transformed his tragedy into triumph.

His mother came up to me and my supportive daughter Starr at the finish line and with tears glistening in her eyes, summed up what we all were thinking. "I'm so proud of Chad," she said. "Chad just achieved the impossible."

MY JOURNAL THOUGHTS ON *Passion*

There are a lot of starters in the world. Who doesn't love to start new and exciting things? Starting is the easy part. The hard part is finishing. It is finishing that separates those with passion from those without it.

What meaningful quest have I left undone because I wasn't willing to suffer and sacrifice for what I desired most?

What unfinished goal has left me feeling unfulfilled and incomplete?

Everyone has specific tasks and dreams and goals that when finished, when completed, when successfully accomplished, dramatically improve the quality of their life. There is nothing so lethal to personal integrity as half-finished tasks.

Those with passion do; those without passion try. When I say, "I'll try," I build in an excuse. If I start but don't finish, I can always say, "Well, I tried," but if I say, "I'll do," I commit to finish no matter what.

"Mission" means to be sent forth. I will take care to do what I was meant and sent forth to do.

There is nothing more fulfilling than taking a dream, a goal, an aspiration—no matter how difficult—and completing it.

I can then sojourn on my path and say, as did He who defined perfect passion, "It is finished."

IDENTIFY AND HONOR A PRACTITIONER OF
Passion

SELECT someone you know whose behavior best reflects the principles of Passion.

WRITE that person's name in the box provided below.

REACH OUT to and teach that person the meaning of "Passion" and explain why he or she personifies this word.

CHAPTER FIVE

Sapere Vedere

The eye is the window of the soul.

— LEONARDO DA VINCI —

The sky was overcast when the airplane lifted off in Miami, and I struck up a conversation with the passenger seated next to me, a gentleman named Sita Patel from India. We were commenting on the dull nature of the day when suddenly the climbing jet broke through the clouds and emerged into sunlight so brilliant we had to pull down the window shade to cut out the glare.

The sudden change sparked a memory for my seat-mate. He turned to me and said, "As a child in Bombay, I remember coming home on a cloudy day, and my mother asked me, 'How was your day?' 'It was not a good day today; it was very dark,' I answered. 'The sun never came out.' And I remember my mother saying to me, 'The sun did come out. The sun always comes out. You just didn't see it. You must learn, my son, to see beyond the clouds.'"

SEEING A WHOLE NEW WORLD

It has been said, "When we change the way we look at things, the things we look at change." Perhaps no one in history personified this better than Leonardo da Vinci, the great Italian artist, inventor, scientist, and designer who foresaw the future hundreds of years ahead of his time. His novel way of looking at things would in due course open up a whole new world of air and sea exploration, while at the same time, Christopher Columbus, his fellow countryman, was opening up another new world with his discovery of America.

Far beyond being the brilliant artist who painted the *Mona Lisa, The Last Supper,* and numerous other enduring masterpieces, da Vinci was also a master innovator. With his keen mind's eye he looked at all around him from unprecedented angles. He studied the genius and simple economy of nature: the way birds fly, the flow of the tides, the human form and its symmetry; virtually nothing escaped his unique gaze. In his studio he left behind his collection of codices—detailed notes and drawings of inventions that centuries later became the bicycle, the glider, the airplane, the helicopter, the tank, the robot, the gyroscope, the life preserver, the double-hulled boat, the parachute, and the crane. He foresaw marvels of engineering and industry the world wouldn't begin to appreciate or develop until long after he was gone. Five hundred–plus years later, the scope of what this quintessential "Renaissance man" envisaged is hard to fathom.

When asked for the secret of his genius, da Vinci would characteristically respond with the phrase he conceived and adopted as his personal motto:

Sapere vedere (pronounced sah-PARE-ay veh-DARE-ay).

The phrase combines the Latin "sapere," which means *knowing how,* and "vedere," which means *to see.*

Sapere vedere is *knowing how to see.* It transposes the

saying, "Seeing is believing" to "Believing is seeing."

People with sapere vedere look forward as well as inward; they are capable of believing and seeing what others don't. Da Vinci understood that we truly see with our brain first, our heart second, and then our eyes. Knowing *how* to see, he realized, is crucial to living a life of significance. It enables us to focus on what we want to see happen instead of focusing on what we don't want to see happen. People without sapere vedere say, "I'll cross that bridge when I get there." Those with sapere vedere say, "I'll see that bridge before I cross it."

Sapere vedere is three dimensional, a combination of hindsight, foresight, and insight.

"Hindsight" is *seeing back*. "Hind" is *behind*. It's where we've been. "Foresight" is *seeing ahead*. "Fore" is *before*. It's what is in front of us. "Insight" is *seeing from within*. It's what we see with the eyes of our mind and feel with the pulse of our heart.

As Myles Munroe writes in his book *The Principles and Power of Vision*, "Sight is a function of the eyes, vision is a function of the heart. . . . Vision sets you free from the limitations of what the eyes can see and allows you to enter into the liberty of what the heart can feel. Never let your eyes determine what your heart believes."

People without vision often fixate on the past. They look at what has happened as a hitching post instead of as a guidepost. By letting only hindsight dictate, they ensure that their path will invariably repeat itself. It is a trademark of those with sapere vedere to see not only the past and present but also the future. By focusing on what's within our heart and mind, and looking ahead, vision pulls us forward.

Afternoons with Arthur

Arthur had a hop in his step the day our word study focused on "vision" and "sapere vedere." The words brought out the kid in him. He was so excited to teach me about them he almost walked past his walker as he raced me to the retirement home's living room.

After we arrived at our destination and settled into our chairs around the fire, Arthur announced as much as questioned, "Did you know that both 'vision' and 'wisdom' are sight words?"

He explained that the words have Old Germanic roots. "Wisdom" comes from "wissen," which means *I know what I saw.* "Vision" comes from "vissen," which means *I know what I see.*

"Wisdom," he continued, "is knowing what we saw. Vision is knowing what we see. And sapere vedere is knowing how to see."

Arthur pointed to the fireplace next to us. The original word for fireplace, he taught, was "hearth," meaning *heart.* In earlier times the hearth was where everything of significance took place. The heat from the home came out of the hearth. The meals that sustained life were prepared in the hearth. Meaningful conversations took place around the hearth. It was the focal point or focus point. It was the center or heart of the home.

Arthur then quoted from Proverbs: "Where there is no vision, the people perish." With vision, people look ahead with confidence. "Confidence" means to *go with faith*. Clear vision allows us to proceed with faith in ourselves.

As Arthur continued to teach, I watched the glee in his eyes and the joy he had as he immersed and lost himself in the secrets of language. He was a picture of contentment. His body was bent and well past its prime, but I realized that with his wisdom and his vision, he could go places in his mind few others could comprehend. Housebound in a retirement home, he was as free as anyone I'd ever known.

I reflected on a study I had recently been shown that found it can be dangerous when people retire without a vision for the future. If their vision was "someday"— someday get a car, someday get a house, someday get the kids out of the house, someday get the gold watch—if that is what they lived for, once they get it and then retire, very often they die within a few short years. Apathy sets in because they have no future path to follow. (Apathy, as Arthur had taught me, is having no path. Goals, dreams, and aspirations disappear. Etymologically, "apathy" means *without feeling or suffering*. It is the antithesis of passion and vision.)

Here in front of me was a man with profound vision. Although I was in good health, with good hearing, excellent eyesight, and boundless opportunities ahead, I found myself envying him.

No Limits

I had just started the Boston Marathon in Hopkington, Massachusetts, when I noticed a runner ahead of me, obviously older than myself, expertly weaving his way through the crowded field of runners. It was the one hundredth anniversary of the venerable marathon, and more than 40,000 runners, including qualifiers and bandits jumping in unofficially, packed the route. Even though organizers, in an effort to manage the crowd, sent out groups in waves, according to qualifying times, once you were on the course, it was like weaving through a New York subway platform trying to catch a train.

I'd noticed the man ahead of me as we awaited the start. He was trim and fit, and he stretched and bounced around like all runners do before they set out on a 26.2-mile marathon. But there was something about him that seemed to set him apart that I couldn't quite identify. Then our group was set loose, and I tried to follow him through the masses. He ran effortlessly, almost as if no one else was there, and quickly he pulled ahead.

It was only then that I noticed the runner alongside him. These two men moved in tandem. When one leaned left, the other leaned left; when one moved right, the other moved right. I increased my pace to get a closer look, and it hit me. The man I'd watched warming up at the start was blind. The runner beside him was his guide; he would direct him with just a touch of his fingers on his elbow. And they were flying! Another couple of minutes, and they were out of sight.

I found out later who the man was. I was talking with a

neighbor about my experience watching the blind runner at the start of the marathon, and he said, "That's got to be Harry Cordellos, probably the world's greatest blind athlete. I have guided him as a ski guide. You should read his book, *No Limits*."

I found the book and read it, and better than that, I had the pleasure of meeting Harry in person when I invited him to stay at our home and speak at a retreat in the Rocky Mountains. Harry was astonishing. He would walk through the forest, inhale deeply, and say, "Hmm, are those lodgepole pines? Are they this tall? This big around?" And he was more often right than wrong.

Here was someone visually impaired, but as the title of his book implied, he had no limitations. Harry once water-skied the thirty-seven miles from Dana Point, California, to Catalina Island on the choppy Pacific Ocean. A sighted person probably couldn't have done it because they would have seen all the obstacles. But Harry just sailed along, just as he had at the Boston Marathon, his inner sight set on his ultimate destination. He knew what his purpose was, and that made all the difference.

YOUR PATH AND PURPOSE

Purpose is the all-important ingredient for sapere vedere. Once we know our purpose, we become pathfinders. Knowing what we want to do dictates where we go and where we put our focus. Our path is the *way* we travel. Our vision is *where* we travel. Our purpose is *why* we travel.

Da Vinci said, "May your work be in keeping with your purpose."

We often say, "You did that on purpose." It means doing what we propose to do. The word "purpose" is a derivative of "propose," an Old English word that is a combination of "pro," which means *forth,* and "pose," which means *to put.* To propose is *to put forth* what we intend to have happen in our life. When we align our lives with what has been proposed, we are answering the clarion call to live "on purpose." We were each created for and with a purpose, just as everything in nature was created for and with a purpose.

As Viktor Frankl said, "Everyone has his own specific vocation or mission in life, everyone must carry out a concrete assignment that demands fulfillment. Therein he cannot be replaced nor can his life be repeated."

Understanding, as well as appreciating, our unique calling is crucial. The two most important days of our life are the day we were born and the day we discover what we were born to do. That's the day we catch the vision of who we are meant to be.

Visualize the Feeling

Peter Vidmar, who won two gold medals as an Olympic gymnast, shared with me his personal experience that illustrates this point. He started training for the Olympics at the age of twelve and didn't compete in the Games until he was twenty-three, eleven long years later. That's a lot of preparation time, an interminable succession of hours in the gym doing the same exercises over and over again. The only way he could stay focused for that long was to constantly visualize the desired end result and connect with his inner emotion.

"I had a vision of what I wanted to become—an Olympic champion," Peter said. "I can't downplay the importance of that. It was really what kept me going."

Seeing himself performing a perfect routine and standing at the top of the podium with a gold medal around his neck wasn't the end-all either. "The question wasn't so much 'How will I *look*?'" he said. "The question was 'How will I *feel*?' That is a much stronger motivator."

Every day at the conclusion of an exhausting six-hour workout, Peter and teammate Tim Daggett would stay in the gym after their teammates had left and visualize themselves in the Olympic finals by conceptualizing exactly what they needed to do in their routines. When the Olympic finals finally did arrive, those two were the last performers for the United States in a tight battle with the team from the People's Republic of China. When Vidmar and Daggett performed nearly perfect routines—the routines they had seen and felt in their minds and hearts for years—the United States got the gold.

Shortly after the Olympics ended, I arranged for Peter to give a speech to our sales team at Franklin about his experiences at the Games and the important role visualizing played in his success. Many times since then I have consulted him when I have needed help visualizing goals and dreams. His ability to not just see with his mind and eyes, but deeply feel with his heart, is invaluable.

SEE IT TO BE IT

It's been said that vision is what we see when we close our eyes. We have to *see it* before we can *be it*. "Dream lofty dreams," wrote James Allen. "And as you dream so shall you become. Your vision is the promise of what you shall one day be."

My friend and business colleague Richard Paul Evans, the *New York Times* bestselling author, recently took me to lunch and shared a compelling story about the immense power of vision. He recalled his early days as a writer when he and his wife, Keri, and their two children lived in a compact 700-square-foot home. He had just completed his first novel, *The Christmas Box,* and it began selling briskly through word of mouth. Seeing a potential that few first-time authors would have the temerity to envision, he set a goal to have the No. 1 book in America. After establishing that lofty target, he promptly went out and bought five gold bracelets for himself and his supporters, who joined him in his commitment to see his book become the country's top-selling book. The bearers of these gold bracelets vowed to leave them on until that goal was achieved.

He told me of the excitement he felt when he placed the bracelet on his wrist and how it served as a consistent, tangible reminder of the vision he had for his book. It was an emotional connection to his goal. Whenever he would shake hands, or write, or pick up the phone, he reconnected to the purpose at hand.

It was with sheer delight that he related to me the incredible feeling and emotional high that he experienced months later when he was featured in *People* magazine as the author of the No. 1 book in America. When he was photographed for the feature article, he held his hand out and pushed his gold bracelet as far forward as he could on his wrist so that the other four bearers of the bracelet could see that their shared vision had been realized. That same scenario was repeated when he appeared as a guest of Katie Couric on the *Today* show. He looked at the camera and held his hand up next to his face and again pushed that gold bracelet to the edge of his wrist, symbolically affirming that dreams really do come true if you feel them and see them clearly enough.

Fifteen million books and fourteen consecutive *New York Times* bestsellers later, Richard Paul Evans remains a firm believer in creating vision that moves you forward. He has since founded an international organization, Christmas Box House International, dedicated to preventing child abuse and protecting battered and abandoned children. He continues to manifest the dreams that he holds in his heart and in his mind.

We are the ones who determine our vision. We decide what we want, what we dream about, what we set our sights on. Gandhi saw a free India. It didn't matter that no one else did. He did. We are free to choose our dreams. There are no limits. Personal prosperity, professional mastery, athletic perfection, family fulfillment, enriching relationships, peace and tranquility, health and wellness, selfless service, leaving a legacy: if we can envision it, we can achieve it.

A Vision Board

John Assaraf, a valued friend, entrepreneur extraordinaire, and one of the teachers from the runaway bestseller *The Secret,* is a master at using vision to create the life of his dreams. Several years ago I was visiting him at his home in San Diego, and he invited me to his office above the garage overlooking the pool and guesthouse. He showed me a vision board that hung on the wall above his desk. On it were pictures he'd cut out of those things he wanted to have and do. He discussed the significance of several of the images, which led to a discussion about the power of the human mind and our natural tendency to seek after goals.

We went back in the main house, and while we were watching his two sons, Noah and Keenan, play, John looked over and asked if he had ever told me how he came to live in this house. I told him he hadn't, and he proceeded to share one of the most amazing accounts of visualization I have ever heard. He explained how his family had moved several times and that some of their belongings had been in storage for years by the time they settled down in this exciting new home. He described how soon after they moved in, he and Keenan had opened up a packing box labeled "vision boards." On it was a picture of the home they were now standing in. It wasn't a picture that looked *like* their new home; it was their *exact* home. John told me he'd cut the photograph out of a luxury home magazine five years earlier while living in Indiana and had glued it on the vision board. At the time he didn't know where his envisioned dream home was located or how much it cost. The vision board had stayed in storage for years, yet he had purchased and was living in the very home he'd visualized. Years after I heard this story, John would share it to illustrate the principle of the law of attraction in *The Secret,* and later in the subsequent book he coauthored, *The Answer,* he showed how to take the action steps to make dreams become reality.

Seeing Beyond Adversity

Visualization is the first key to a successful future. The best way to predict the future is to see it and then create it by doing it. It was the sculptor Michelangelo, a countryman of da Vinci, who said, "In every block of marble I see a statue as plain as though it stood before me, shaped and perfect in attitude and action. I have only to hew away the rough walls that imprison the lovely apparition to reveal it to the other eyes as mine see it."

Sometimes the marble we chisel as we face hurdles and challenges in our individual lives is malleable, and sometimes it's hard. However difficult, being able to see what is ahead unleashes the ability to persevere and prevail.

A remarkable example of this is the life of a contemporary sculptor, Gary Lee Price. Because of his unique skills and gifts, Gary was commissioned to sculpt the Statue of Responsibility as envisioned by Viktor Frankl, a monument that will one day complement the Statue of Liberty. The prototype sculpture Gary has created shows two hands firmly gripped together, one reaching from below, the other from above, together symbolizing the responsibility we share with one another.

While in Austria to show a model of the statue to Dr. Frankl's family, this gifted artist talked about his own personal journey through the grip of adversity.

Being in Europe, he said, brought back deep personal memories that were excruciatingly painful and yet warmly reassuring that all great accomplishments start with dreams.

Gary was just six years old when he lived with his mother and stepfather in U.S. military housing in Germany, where his stepfather was stationed. He recalled how his mother first noticed his gift for drawing and encouraged him as a young child to develop that talent. "She would hold my hand and teach me how to make strokes with crayon and pencil," said Gary. "She frequently told me I had a gift. She praised me and assured me that I would create great works of art."

Then one night, hours after he had gone to sleep, Gary awoke in his bed to screaming and shouting. All these years later, he recounted in acrid detail how he ran into the room, just as his stepfather leveled a gun at his mother and squeezed the trigger. He watched his mother's bright eyes close as she died in front of him and then watched in more horror as his stepfather turned the gun on himself. It would be years, Gary acknowledged, before he would be able to successfully move beyond that traumatic experience. But over time, and with maturity, he realized the enduring part of his mother's memory wasn't her tragic death, but the vision she held for him: that he truly had a gift to be a great artist, and he should never, no matter what, stop pursuing that gift.

Becoming acquainted with the life of Viktor Frankl, a man who refused to be defeated by the humiliation of Nazi brutality, only enhanced Gary's appreciation for the importance of accepting life on its terms and finding meaning because of those terms, not in spite of them.

"I wouldn't change my life," he said. "I, like Viktor, am an optimist. There is not one thing I would change in my life or cancel during those years of tragedy and suffering. Why? Because I like who I have become and what I am blessed with and enjoy on a daily basis. Any pain or past suffering has helped mold and form me into a person who can promote good in the world. Through my awareness as an artist, I create sculpture that lifts and inspires others."

Gary was able to build on his mother's vision for him, and now his artwork is displayed in some of the most prominent locations and prestigious galleries in the world.

Gary demonstrates genuine resilience in his life. "Resilience" is derived from the Latin word "resilire." "Re" means *back,* and "salire" is *to leap.* When we are resilient, we *leap back* up after getting knocked down. If we are unable to rebound from setbacks and disappointments, we will never be able to visualize our true potential.

HARNESSING ADVERSITY

Bad things happen to all of us at one time or another. Anyone who has senses, who breathes, touches, feels, smells, tastes, has had to endure something difficult, something trying, something so awful that it seems to have the ability to snuff out life itself. As we walk our path and seek to fulfill our purpose, we will inevitably have disappointments that knock us down.

In his pioneering work on adversity and resilience, *Adversity Quotient: Turning Obstacles into Opportunities*, Dr. Paul Stoltz suggests we can do one of two things when adversity crosses our path. We can view our life as if we are in a pit, as if the rug has been pulled out from underneath and we're in this deep hole we can't quite get out of. Or we can maintain clear vision of what our life is about, know what our purpose is, and harness that adversity to launch us onto higher ground.

If we have a strong and clear enough picture, if we don't merely see with our eyes, but feel with our hearts and reason in our minds, we can and will overcome anything.

LIVE LIFE IN CRESCENDO

As with anything worthwhile, viewing life through the clear lens of sapere vedere requires consistency and diligence.

Dr. Stephen R. Covey, a trusted mentor, recently shared with me his personal motto that serves to keep his vision clear.

That motto: *Live life in crescendo.*

I asked him what that means.

"To live life in crescendo is to constantly look forward. It means that your greatest work, and contribution, is always ahead of you. The philosophy places the emphasis on contribution. While achievement has a beginning and an end, contribution is ongoing and enduring.

"If you focus on contribution and not on achievement," he concluded, "you will achieve more than your wildest dreams."

Interestingly enough, "crescendo" is a derivative of "crescere," a word that originated in the eighteenth century, which means *to increase* or *grow*. The language is Italian.

Da Vinci would be proud.

MY JOURNAL THOUGHTS ON *Sapere Vedere*

It is a crystal clear day in Dana Point, and I can see Catalina Island in the distance.

I'm reminded of a story about a remarkable woman by the name of Florence Chadwick who on July 4, 1952, waded into the water off Catalina Island intending to become the first woman to swim from the island to the coast of California. Fifteen hours into her attempt, dense fog rolled in, and she began to doubt her ability to go on. Buoyed by the encouragement of her mother and trainer riding alongside in a support boat, she continued on for nearly an hour before finally succumbing to fatigue and exhaustion. The fog lifted soon after Florence was pulled from the water, revealing the shore less than a half mile away.

Hours later she lamented to a reporter, "If I could have seen land, I know I would have made it!"

Florence tried again two months later, this time with a clear picture of the coastline imprinted on her heart and mind. Despite the same dense fog, she became the first woman to swim the Catalina Channel, eclipsing the men's record by two hours.

I would not want to embark on a journey unless I could see my way clear to the end.

Clarity empowers. Henry David Thoreau invited, "Go confidently in the direction of your dreams."

Creating a clear image of an end result empowers its achievement. Once I _See It_, I will _Be It_, and _Do It_, and in due course, I will _Have It_.

As Aristotle taught, "The soul never thinks without a picture." As I model to the universe that I know how to see, the universe will see to it that my dreams are fulfilled.

IDENTIFY AND HONOR A PRACTITIONER OF
Sapere Vedere

SELECT someone you know whose behavior best reflects Sapere Vedere.

WRITE that person's name in the box provided below.

REACH OUT to and teach that person the meaning of "Sapere Vedere" and explain why he or she personifies these words.

CHAPTER SIX

humility

To keep a lamp burning we have to keep putting oil in it.

— MOTHER TERESA —

Humility is one of the most misunderstood and misapplied words in all of language. Humility is not being passive and submissive, nor is it distinguished by slumping shoulders, bowed heads, and subservient, downward glances. It is about being teachable and coachable. It implies a continual commitment to learning and growing and expanding. It is living life in crescendo, with shoulders back and heads up as we reach and stretch to become our very best, then extend ourselves to help others do the same. And then, we start again!

Humility is the hub of the wheel, the solid core between self-mastery and leadership. It is here, in the middle of this book, to connect the words of the first five chapters—words for self-discovery and personal development—with the words featured in the final five chapters—words that empower us to help, inspire, and potentially lead others. We can't influence until we've been influenced. We can't change the world until we are changed.

Through humility this transition can happen.

The origin of "humility" is the Latin word "humus" meaning *soil,* specifically rich, dark, organic soil. When a seed is planted in fertile soil, it transforms into something far greater. The acorn becomes the oak tree. The smallest of seeds carefully planted in the spring becomes the bounteous harvest in the fall. It all starts with the nurturing quality of the soil—humus.

When we have sufficient humus in our lives, we grow and develop, and foster those around us to flourish. Humility produces growth.

THE KEY TO GROWTH

Growth can occur in a variety of ways. Abundance is seldom produced through sterile and hardened soil. A fruitful crop is rarely the product of an unattended and overgrown garden. We can grow and learn by unlearning, by letting go of something old in order to make room for something new. There are times to add extra nutrients to cultivate growth. A plentiful harvest is preceded by careful plowing, planting, and pruning.

When we develop our gifts, we in effect unwrap and unfold them for the benefit of all, including ourselves. Our gifts and talents increase as we nurture our nature. In contrast, when we feign to know it all, we close off promising opportunities to develop and expand our gifts. A garden reciprocates the love and care it receives from the gardener. To develop yourself is to love yourself.

Limitless possibilities await those who have the humility to admit they don't know it all. Prosperity is found by cultivating an attitude of lifelong learning.

"Success" and "humility" are terms not commonly used interchangeably, yet the two words are intimately linked. As with "humility," the etymological roots of "success" can be traced back to the soil. "Success" comes from the Latin "succeder" and means *to come up through.* The middle part of the word, "cede," is an offshoot of "seed." When a seed pushes through the dirt, or humus, into the daylight, it follows a path of success and succession. To come up through is to succeed. And the only way to come up through is to take advantage of the rich humus. We plant seeds of success by getting grounded and rooted in humility. There is no real humility without success and no real success without humility.

Afternoons with Arthur

I remember the afternoon Arthur unwittingly taught me about humility and reinforced how it is never too late to embark on a journey of self-improvement. I was running late for our scheduled word study session. When I finally arrived at the retirement home and walked down the hall toward Arthur's room, there he was, sitting on a chair out in the hallway, waiting for me. He was reading a book. I looked at the title as he closed the cover: *Spellbound.* It was, on the surface, a riveting title, suggesting a mystery book, perhaps, or some other kind of suspense thriller.

Then I read the subtitle: *The Surprising Origins and Astonishing Secrets of English Spelling.*

Here was the greatest etymologist I'd ever met, a wordsmith of no equal, and even in his nineties he was reading a book about spelling. The professor is, and always will be, a student first.

I kidded him as we walked into his "office"—the recliner in the corner of his room—about his choice of reading material. Without missing a beat, Arthur responded, "Mastery is a lifelong pursuit."

He proceeded to talk about the word "master," and in a way that only he could, he brought it to life by explaining its early usage. He had a gift for taking words that are easily recognizable and in common usage and uncovering their original meaning that had been obscured by the layers of time.

A master didn't become a master overnight, he explained. There was a process. First, one must become an apprentice, then a journeyman, and finally a master.

Apprentice. Journeyman. Master. These three words illustrate the importance of going through fundamental and necessary steps to acquire the kind of humility that is commensurate with true leadership.

Arthur grew quite animated as if he were about to reveal an ancient truth. "Do you know that 'apprentice' means *learner*?" he asked, then taught that the word comes from the French "apprendre," which means *to learn.*

In earlier times, he recounted, apprentice was the name for someone who would select a trade, then find a master in his village to teach him the skills necessary for his chosen vocation. After learning all he could from the local master, the apprentice would then travel elsewhere to broaden his education. Launching forward on such a journey turned an apprentice into a journeyman. A journeyman would often travel long distances for the privilege of working under that master who could best help him further hone his craft. Over time, a journeyman could eventually become a master himself—and be in a position to start the cycle all over again.

"But a master never stops learning," Arthur pointed out. "No matter how many journeymen he might instruct, a true master continues to enlarge and expand his own craft to his dying day."

No one epitomized mastery more than the master I was speaking with. When he was a full professor and head of his university's language department, he once took a sabbatical to enroll as a student at Georgetown University, where he studied Latin and Greek from a renowned Jesuit priest.

In his study, Arthur would recount such experiences the way a baseball player might recollect home runs. On a summer trip to Norway, he recalled, he knocked on the door at the University of Oslo and asked when they offered courses in Norwegian. They explained that they had a course for beginners in the morning, a course for intermediates in the afternoon, and an advanced course in the evening. "Great," Arthur said. "I'll take all three." Remarkably, within a few short months after returning he had written and published a textbook on learning Norwegian.

Arthur's unslakable thirst for knowledge has allowed him to thrive into the winter of his life. He epitomizes the meaning of the word "master," and I reflect often on how fortunate I am to be his "apprentice."

EARNERS ARE LEARNERS

Arthur's words reminded me of a study we conducted when I was head of the sales and training division at Franklin. We wanted to find out what separated our top producers, those who made several hundred thousand dollars a year, from those who made a tenth of that. What made them unique? What set them apart? What differentiated a master sales professional, a high earner, from a minimum earner?

We brought in an outside consulting firm to determine the difference, and after hours of interviews and weeks of research the consultants summed up their discoveries in three words: earners are learners.

Our top performers, without exception, were avid and devoted learners. They were constantly taking in new information and using it. We found that they each read over two dozen books a year. They were tireless in educating themselves in a variety of topics—especially about the needs of their clients. It seems as though they knew their clients better than their clients knew themselves. Our top salespeople knew our product line inside and out, as well as the specific features and benefits of each of those products. Even though they were at the very top of their profession, the people everyone else in the company either looked up to or envied, none of them thought they knew it all. They demonstrated humility by continually seeking to learn more, aspiring to always move to a new level of experience and expertise.

A Humble Leader

While working as a consultant in the hospitality industry, I made the acquaintance of Norman Brinker, an unassuming multimillionaire and restaurateur extraordinaire. Nothing about Norman suggested his abundant wealth and enormous influence. He was neither imperious nor aloof. I found myself in his home in Dallas one Monday morning, invited there for breakfast before I caught a flight later that day.

I knew Norman's story. He grew up practically penniless in Roswell, New Mexico. His first job was as a newpaper boy, delivering papers by bicycle, then by horse, and eventually by car as his rural route expanded. Somehow he went from that modest beginning to a life of iconic accomplishment. He was an Olympic equestrian and also competed in the modern pentathlon, an event that involves running, shooting, horseback riding, fencing, and swimming, at the world championships. He became a legendary philanthropist. And as a businessman and pioneer in founding the casual dining industry, he had few peers.

Norman always inspired me with his enthusiasm and zest for life. There wasn't one phase of his life where he didn't seem to jump in with both feet.

On that day I had a long list of questions catalogued in my mind that I wanted to ask the great Norman Brinker. How did he revolutionize the restaurant industry? How did he turn a handful of restaurants into the multibillion-dollar Brinker International, the holding company of such popular chains as Chili's, Romano's Macaroni Grill,

On The Border Mexican Grill, and Maggiano's Little Italy? How did he create a company culture so vibrant, innovative, and relevant? How did he know that Americans would respond so eagerly to sitting down and eating in a casual dining environment? How and why did he envision the first salad bar? How did he retrofit his Chili's restaurants to serve sizzling fresh fajitas? How did his involvement garner such widespread support for the launch of the Susan G. Komen Breast Cancer Foundation, one of the most successful nonprofit organizations in the world?

But I couldn't get a question in. Why? Because Norman was asking all the questions. He wanted to know about my life, about my goals and dreams, about my interests and accomplishments. He was as inquisitive as a curious child.

His close friends and associates attested that he was that way with everyone he met—never domineering or autocratic; a man far more interested in others than in himself; a man who listened more than he spoke. He lifted himself by lifting others; he improved himself by improving others.

Dozens of executives who apprenticed under him and observed his humble leadership have used his example to parallel his success. These CEOs now lead publicly traded companies like Chili's, Outback Steakhouse, P. F. Chang's, Buca di Beppo, T.G.I. Friday's, and Pei Wei Asian Diner, to name just a few. They have one thing in common: they all sprang from the fertile soil that was Norman Brinker's life.

The Habit of Humility

One of the great master teachers in my life is Dr. Stephen R. Covey. He is the one who taught me that humility is the "Mother of all Virtues." His generous and affirming support have been instrumental in the development of this book. He embodies so many facets of this precious jewel of the earth we call humility. While discussing a unique word or meaning, it is not unusual to hear him inquire, "How do you spell that word? What does it mean again? Where did it come from?"

Although Stephen is widely regarded as one of the top thought leaders of our day, he still recognizes the need for private, internal victories achieved through daily self-development and mastery. It is not uncommon to enter his home and find piles of books in his study, family room, kitchen, even next to the bathtub. These paper cairns mark the path of an assiduous reader who often scans a book or more each day. Again corroborating the results of our research of our sales team at Franklin, readers are leaders, and leaders are readers.

The man *Time* magazine recognized as "one of the twenty-five most influential Americans" of our time emulates daily how an influencer first needs to be influenced. The man who taught us *The 7 Habits of Highly Effective People* has made humility the core habit of his life.

Living life in crescendo is much more than a mere motto for Stephen. He's in the autumn of his life, and he's still speaking, teaching, learning, and practicing humility every single day. It is a habit. It is a way of living and learning and constantly improving. It is humility. And it should come as no surprise that a fellow cultivator of humus, Norman Brinker, attributed much of his professional success to the powerful lessons taught firsthand by a master teacher by the name of Stephen Covey.

To teach is *to show*. You can't teach what you don't know. You can't guide where you don't go. And you can't grow what you don't sow.

PLANT THE SEED

Dr. Gerald Bell's serendipitous appearance on my path in the wilds of Wyoming, as I mentioned earlier, led to several conversations between us that taught me about the link between humility and goal setting. His exhaustive study of retired executives—he called it his "Study of 4,000"—took thousands of hours to conduct and complete. Those surveyed averaged seventy years of age, and when asked what they would do differently if they could live their lives over again, they responded with deep remorse for not having a better plan for their life. The responses he received were telling: "I would have carved out life goals and owned my life." "Life is not practice, it is the real thing." "I should have taken charge of my life through goal setting." "I would have spent more time on my personal development." "I would have planned my career better."

Planning requires intent and preparation. To plan is *to plant*. We must first plant a seed if it is to ever have a chance to grow. Contrary to popular opinion, it takes true humility to first plan and to then follow through and achieve worthwhile goals. Those married to false humility—not going after what they deserve, not measuring up to their potential, not acknowledging the full measure of their talents—endure humiliation, the very antithesis of humility.

BEGINNER'S MIND

In the East, great masters have developed an acuity they call the "beginner's mind." In the martial arts world, a black belt, the symbol that the West commonly associates with great accomplishment, signifies a serious beginner. Perspective is described with a single word: "shoshin." The word and its ancient symbol, 初心, depict an attitude of openness and eagerness. The Zen teacher Shunryo Suzuki-roshi explained, "In the beginner's mind there are many possibilities, but in the expert's there are few." Practitioners of shoshin pledge to bring no preconceptions when studying a subject. Even at an advanced level they approach the subject as a beginner would.

Developing shoshin requires time and patience and a willingness to listen, observe, and learn from those who appear on our path. In Vienna, where Pravin Cherkoori taught me the word "Genshai," he proclaimed, "Isn't life magical! Look at what happens when you view yourself as an empty bucket and every person you meet as a well—and you put your bucket under the tap that draws from that well. All the nutrients that sustain life and produce growth flow right into your bucket."

MY JOURNAL THOUGHTS ON *Humility*

I change as I confront and conquer challenges.

To change is to <u>bend</u> or <u>adapt</u>.

A once dormant seed transforms into a seedling that bends and turns as it pushes through the earth to fulfill its purpose.

Challenges create change, and change promotes growth.

Setting goals is a way to purposely create challenges.

Goals, like water, have the power to sustain me. Well-planned goals empower me to go over, under, and around obstacles.

Gifts and talents provide the fuel for goal achievement, but unless a gift is developed, it deteriorates. It's the law of atrophy: use it or lose it. Atrophy means <u>wasting away</u>. Talents, like muscles, waste away from lack of use. When muscles are challenged and strained, they grow stronger.

Resist and expand . . . _Change and grow_ . . . _stretch and develop_ . . . That is the true essence of humility.

By identifying the specific gifts I would most like to expand, I will embark on a journey of self-mastery and make my life a masterpiece.

As the English playwright Philip Massinger taught, "He that would govern others, first should be Master of himself."

IDENTIFY AND HONOR AN EXAMPLE OF

Humility

SELECT someone you know whose behavior best reflects true Humility.

WRITE that person's name in the box provided below.

REACH OUT to and teach that person the meaning of "Humility" and explain why he or she personifies this word.

CHAPTER SEVEN

INSPIRE

In everyone's life, at some time, our inner fire goes out.
It is then burst into flame by an encounter
with another human being.

— ALBERT SCHWEITZER —

Art Berg looked to be a most unlikely source of inspiration when he rolled his wheelchair into the training room of the Baltimore Ravens.

It was late summer of 2000, and members of the National Football League team were in the middle of two-a-days, that grueling part of training camp when each day two practices are held, morning and after-noon, in preparation for the punishing regular season ahead.

Art had been summoned by then Ravens' head coach Brian Billick to talk to the team before that morning's workout. It wasn't yet eight o'clock when he took a posi-tion in the front of the room, facing a collection of large men slumped into folding chairs, in varying degrees of consciousness, ice packs and Ace bandages taped to their knees and ankles. Their body language, as much as they were communicating at this time of the morning, screamed indifference. Their faces looked ahead blankly. Since childhood, these men had heard such speeches, designed to motivate them to get more out of their sig-nificant physical talents. What could this man sitting in a wheelchair possibly tell them that they hadn't already heard? How could he inspire them more than they'd already been inspired?

Then Art told them his story: how he was on his way to be married when he was in the accident that left him a quadriplegic. How he had to fight through years of challenges and pain and setbacks just to get released from the hospital and marry the woman of his dreams. How he needed to relearn the most basic of human chores—brushing his teeth, putting on his shoes—without the use of his arms and legs. How he had to endure setbacks and disappointment and develop a kind of patience he had no idea existed.

He was twenty-one when it happened, not much younger than most of the players. One minute he was a passenger in a car speeding across the Nevada desert, the next the car was flipping end over end, each revolution further ensuring the robust, athletic, physical life he knew was gone. When he awoke in the hospital, the opening of his eyelids exceeded all other movement. He willed himself to crawl a half inch at a time. It would be months before he could even get into a wheelchair, months more before he could move it forward at all.

When times got darkest, he told them, he read a poem from an English author, William Ernest Henley, that silenced that incessant inner voice of doom that assured him all was lost.

The poem, entitled "Invictus," included this stanza:

It matters not how strait the gate,
How charged with punishments the scroll,

I am the master of my fate:
I am the captain of my soul.

"It's up to you to decide what you want to accomplish," Art challenged the football players that morning. "You and you alone." His goal when he awoke bent and broken in the hospital, surrounded by all the abundant reasons he couldn't do anything, was to become a champion at all the things he could do. He could become independent. He could marry his sweetheart. He could have a family. He could drive his own car and run his own life. He could write books that would help and inspire others. He could become one of the country's most sought-after inspirational speakers and be in a position to remind enormously gifted athletes that they could be anything they wanted to be. He could, and he did.

INVICTUS

The Ravens were coming off a mediocre season, and there were plenty of reasons—injuries, personnel problems, other teams with supposedly superior talent—to presume this season wouldn't be any different. But that didn't mean they had to accept an outcome others had prescribed for them. That didn't mean they couldn't overcome all the reasons *why not*. Art defined "invictus," a Latin word that stands for *unconquered, unsubdued, invincible.* If your goal is to win the Super Bowl and be crowned as the best team in football, Art stressed, *you* are the master of that fate.

As the players quietly filed out of the room, Art wasn't

sure how his message had been received. The owner of the team asked him to stay and watch a preseason game before he flew home. The Ravens fell behind by a large margin. The owner turned to Art and said, "If we somehow come back, I'm going to put 'Invictus' on the scoreboard."

Digging deep, the Ravens charged back and won the game, and then, with "Invictus" as their rallying cry, the team began the regular season by winning five of its first six games.

But after that they lost their focus and dropped three straight games.

The Ravens sent out a distress signal to Art Berg. "We wonder if you could come back and talk to the team again," Coach Billick said.

Art and his wheelchair flew to Baltimore and met a much more receptive audience than the one that greeted him in training camp. The players assembled in front of him were eager for his words. They had listened to his message of encouragement before, but *now* they were really listening.

Art reminded them of the power of invictus. He reinforced his keys for success. Don't listen to the critics. Don't pay attention to all the reasons why you can't reach your goal. Concentrate on your strengths, not your weaknesses. It is your call. Be unconquered, unsubdued, invincible. Invictus.

The Baltimore Ravens won every game in the remainder of the season, and in the playoffs they continued to be unconquerable. When the smoke had cleared at the Super Bowl, the scoreboard read Baltimore 34, New York

7. Against long odds, innumerable critics, and their own private doubts when the season began, the Baltimore Ravens were champions of the football world.

After the Super Bowl triumph, Art was summoned to Baltimore yet again, but not as a speaker this time. It was the team's award banquet, and the players had something they wanted him to have—his own Super Bowl ring. The man who couldn't move his arms or legs but inspired them to a world championship was their most valuable player. To prove it was a single word engraved on each side of their Super Bowl rings: INVICTUS.

A TRUE INSPIRATION

I met Art Berg shortly after the accident that rendered him paralyzed, and I watched as he transformed himself into the champion who positively impacted everything, and everyone, he touched.

It was Art who inspired Chad Hymas, the young man whose story we met in Chapter 4, to manage his own paralysis and reach his personal goals. Two months before the accident that cost Chad the use of his arms and legs, Art was giving a speech at a business convention in Texas. In the audience was Kelly Hymas, Chad's father. Kelly was so moved by Art's message that he bought a copy of his book prior to catching a plane for home.

When Chad woke up paralyzed in the hospital, Kelly made sure a copy of Art's book, *The Impossible Just Takes a Little Longer,* was next to the bed. After reading the book, Chad wrote Art and asked him if he would come to the hospital for a visit. Days later, unannounced, Art rolled his wheelchair into the quadriplegic unit of the hospital where Chad and others were recuperating.

Without a word, Art hopped out of his chair onto a bed and proceeded to demonstrate how a quadriplegic got dressed in the morning. Using his arms and chin and other body contortions his audience had neither imagined nor considered, he was taking off his clothes and putting them back on in front of them, at a speed not to be believed. *You can do this too!* was the message he delivered.

"It was the most amazing thing," Chad marveled. "He just showed up, unannounced, and started doing things we all thought were impossible." From that moment on Chad saw the world in a different, and much brighter, light. The future suddenly looked promising, the possibilities again endless. A man living under no different circumstances than his own, faced with the same daunting obstacles and restrictions, had shown him horizons he didn't know existed.

Art died not long after meeting Chad, due to complications from medications required to keep his paralyzed body functioning. In tribute to Art's life, Chad resolved to do all he could to emulate his mentor's example and try to serve and inspire others as well as Art had served and inspired him. When Chad rolled his wheelchair 513 miles, it was Art's record of 325 miles that he broke. He bought Art's customized van to get around on his own. And he worked tirelessly to become a public speaker who could provide for his family the way Art had provided for his.

After years of paying his dues, the National Speakers

Association designated Chad Hymas a certified speaking professional, a status awarded to only a handful of America's top speakers, including Art Berg.

Everywhere Chad speaks, he pays tribute to his mentor, and whenever he is referred to as a *motivational* speaker, he quickly corrects that designation.

"I am an *inspirational* speaker," he insists. And he was taught to be one by the very best.

Afternoons with Arthur

Arthur took a deep breath. Then he held it in. I wasn't sure what point he was trying to get across, but I was relieved when he exhaled and started breathing normally.

He was teaching me the meaning of the word "inspire," which comes from the Latin "inspirare." "Spirare," he instructed, means *to breathe,* and "in" implies *into.* To inspire is *to breathe into.*

The Master of Words explained that when we breathe life into another, we inspire their hopes, goals, and dreams. We breathe life into them, just as our Creator first breathed life into our spirit.

But when we take the air out of another, we expire their hopes, goals, and dreams.

So we can breathe life in or suck life out—inspire or expire, the choice is ours.

I was constantly amazed at Arthur's ability to bring life to words, and at the ability words had to bring life to him. Our afternoon sessions would invariably begin with Arthur sitting comfortably in his favorite chair, peacefully relaxing. When I mentioned the word "inspire," he became instantly animated, waving his hands and arms as he acted out the definition—the very picture of energy and enthusiasm.

After he illustrated the meaning of "inspire" for me by holding his breath, Arthur moved on to talk about a related word. That word was "encourage." "Coeur" in the Romance languages means *heart,* he explained, gesturing at his own heart. When you "encourage," you *add to someone's heart.* And when you "discourage," you *take away from someone's heart.*

Those who inspire and encourage, Arthur continued, can be thought of as appreciators, those who add value, while those who expire and discourage can be thought of as depreciators, those who lower value.

Arthur noted that words like "appreciate" that begin with "ap," such as "approve," "apply," and "applaud," generally mean *up* or *toward.* And words that begin with "de," like "depreciate," "destroy," "denigrate," and "degrade," generally mean *down* or *away.* Those who appreciate their unique talents and gifts, as well as those of others, create an upward cycle that lifts all in its vortex. Those who depreciate those same talents and gifts spin that cycle in a downward direction.

In every encounter we have with another human being, we have the profound opportunity to either add to their heart or rip out a part of their heart. Words are the currency in our human exchanges. The skill we are able to develop with the appropriate use of words can give us great power and influence.

A Garment of Praise

Said the poet Maya Angelou, "I've learned that people will forget what you said, people will forget what you did, but people will never forget how you made them feel."

In his bestselling book *The Power of Intention*, Wayne Dyer writes about the effect of kindness on the human body. Scientists who studied the brain activity of individuals as they performed an act of kindness for another found increased levels of serotonin, the chemical the brain produces to make you feel good and the common ingredient in antidepressant medication. That wasn't all they found. In those *receiving* the acts of kindness, researchers recorded the same amount of serotonin as that found in those *giving* the service. It was further determined that even those *observing* the acts of kindness produced the same amount of serotonin.

Inspiring environments are contagious. Few things feel more blissful than emerging from cold into warmth. When we inspire and praise others, it is as if we are bringing them out of the cold and wrapping them in a warm "garment of praise."

There is a scene indelibly imprinted on my mind. I was bicycling late one night through Doheny State Park, a stretch of beach on the Pacific with picnic benches and fire pits. At one of these sites a family was gathered to celebrate the birthday of a young boy. A roaring fire lit up the faces of a dozen or so family members as they stood in a circle. In the center of them was a birthday cake emblazoned with candles. Then my gaze fell to the focal point of everyone's attention and admiration: the birthday boy. His face was aglow, lit up like the candles on his cake and the embers burning in the bonfire. There was no mistaking that look. It was one of pure, unadulterated joy and affirmation. I kept looking back as I pedaled away, my own heart warmed as if I were around that fire myself and part of that birthday celebration.

The word "praise" comes from the Old French "preiser" which means *price* or *value*. When we praise others, we add value to them, to their lives, to their dreams. We attach a high price to their efforts and purpose. Our institutions of higher learning bestow recognition on those who graduate at the very top of the class. The title magna cum laude means *with great praise,* and summa cum laude means *with highest praise.* Graduates armed with that kind of praise leave school with feelings of great value.

INSPIRE OR EXPIRE

In his groundbreaking book *The Hidden Messages in Water,* the researcher Masaru Emoto posits the theory that water exposed to positive thoughts and words forms beautiful crystals, whereas water exposed to negative thoughts and words forms distorted crystals. Through the use of high-speed photography, Emoto shows how water appears to change its expression according to the nature of the written or spoken words to which it is exposed.

Over a half century ago Napoleon Hill taught this

timeless principle: "All thought has a tendency to clothe itself in its physical equivalent."

We learned as children that "sticks and stones may break my bones, but words can never hurt me." But that's not true. *Sticks and stones may break my bones, but words can break my heart.*

Words have tremendous power for good or for ill. They can inspire or expire. The choice is ours. We can:

Choose to heal or choose to wound.
Choose to affirm or choose to reject.
Choose to inspire or choose to expire.
Choose to praise or choose to criticize.
Choose to appreciate or choose to depreciate.
Choose to encourage or choose to discourage.
Choose to focus on strengths or choose to focus on weaknesses.

Using words and language that lift the human spirit creates a new paradigm in thinking. Instead of "What can I *get*?" our mentality shifts to "What can I *give*?"

THE REMARKABLE HEART

Our bodies are wired for life, and it all starts with the heart. If we could lay out end to end the vast network of arteries, veins, and capillaries that make up our cardiovascular system, it would cover some 60,000 miles—enough distance to wrap around the earth more than twice. Yet the heart has the ability to take a single red blood cell and circulate it through the entire body in twenty seconds.

The more it is exercised, the stronger the heart becomes. A well-trained athlete's heart can grow 70 percent larger than a normal-sized heart. Conversely, lack of exercise causes the heart muscle to shrink.

But it is more than a pump. It is the key to wellness. The heart is the seat of our deepest emotions and loftiest aspirations. It is at the center of literature dating back to medieval times. Novelists, playwrights, poets, and songwriters through the ages have created their own vocabulary around the heart. Words and phrases such as "heartless," "bighearted," "coldhearted," "heartfelt," and "with all your heart" evoke strong mental images.

In ancient Egypt, the heart was viewed as the seed of humanity. Judaism views the heart as the temple of the soul and the seat of wisdom. In Christianity, the heart is a symbol of love and compassion.

ADDING TO THE HEART

Our family gained a deep personal appreciation for the meaning of "encourage"—*to add to someone's heart*—shortly after our first granddaughter, Taylor, was born. From all outward appearances, Taylor was a healthy baby girl. But a day after her birth, doctors discovered she had a congenital heart defect. Hours of tests followed, resulting in a diagnosis that this new little miracle had a condition called tetralogy of Fallot. It is the most common cause of blue baby syndrome, a condition that can be fatal. In common terms, she had an enlarged heart. In addition to an oversized heart chamber, there was a hole between the bottom two ventricles of her heart, as well as a valve that closed instead of opened every time her heart pumped. As a result, her lungs were not getting the required oxygen.

Nothing had prepared our family for such news. Taylor's parents were both elite athletes. Her mother, our oldest daughter, Summer, was a college soccer player, and her father, Bryson, is a professional cyclist. At the Olympic Training Center in Colorado Springs, his physiological tests graded out at the highest levels. It did not compute that the firstborn of such fit, aerobically gifted parents could have a problem with her heart. But she did.

Surgery was scheduled for six months, when she would be strong enough to handle the stress. On the appointed day, we reported as a family to the hospital. Only one desire filled our heavy hearts: make her whole. We smiled and waved goodbye as she was carried into surgery in the arms of a nurse dressed in scrubs with a cow pattern, a fun camouflage that disguised the seriousness of the situation, just as the smile on Taylor's face camouflaged the troubles hidden in her own tiny heart.

The doctors estimated the operation would last two to three hours. But there were unexpected complications with the heart–lung bypass machine, causing Taylor's body to swell up, and two or three hours soon doubled.

After several anxious hours, a sweaty, beleaguered surgeon with a heart full of emotion slowly walked into the waiting room. He looked as if he'd been run through a wringer. He explained about the life-threatening complication that had caused the extensive delay and how eventually the surgical team was able to add a donor valve, the bicuspid, into Taylor's besieged heart. They trimmed down the valve and delicately attached it to her heart, then sewed in a Gortex-like piece to patch the hole in the bottom of her heart. The relieved doctor said Taylor would now be able to get the healthy oxygen she so desperately needed. These encouraging words allowed Summer, her own heart swollen with pain and fear and love, to finally exhale a breath of hope.

When Taylor was rolled into the intensive care recovery unit, we were not prepared for what we saw. This beautiful infant looked like a balloon, hardly to be recognized. The sight of it backed us all up to the wall. But as we watched Summer rush to her firstborn, never to leave her side until she was better, we realized the importance of what had just happened. If not for the addition to her heart, if not for the skill and knowledge of these expert surgeons and nurses, she wouldn't have survived for long.

As we watch our precious Taylor run and bike and play soccer, we are grateful for every step, pedal, and kick. Most important, we are thankful she is with us and enriches our lives so much. Is it meaningful to add to someone's heart or breathe life into another? *We know it is.*

My Journal Thoughts on *Inspire*

Inspire—<u>Breathe</u>!
Encourage—<u>Add Heart</u>!
<u>Leave others better</u>!

My mother ingrained in me the importance of encouraging and inspiring those who appear on my path. "Leave them better for having met you," she taught.

Without exception, I was expected to treat others large, while treating others small was tantamount to familial treason.

The French philosopher and Jesuit priest Teilhard de Chardin taught, "We are not human beings having a spiritual experience. We are spiritual beings having a human experience."

I can breathe life into the spirit of others.

It has been said, "A friend is someone who knows the song in your heart and can sing it back to you when you have forgotten the words."

I can encourage those I love to think and live big. I can challenge them to go after big dreams and magnify their unique talents.

The fourteenth Dalai Lama taught, "We are visitors on this planet. We are here for ninety or one hundred years at the very most. During that period we must try to do something good, something useful, with our lives. If we contribute to other people's happiness, we will find the true goal, the true meaning of life."

From this day on I resolve to leave every person I meet better for having met me.

IDENTIFY AND HONOR A PERSON WHO
Inspires

SELECT someone you know whose behavior is Inspiring.

WRITE that person's name in the box provided below.

REACH OUT to and teach that person the meaning of "Inspire" and explain why he or she personifies this word.

CHAPTER EIGHT

empathy

To be able to put oneself in another's position,
to be able to see and feel as another person does,
that is the rare gift.

Mata Amritanandamayi

Larry Hall had never heard of a five-step approach, let alone attempted one, when he took a fourteen-pound bowling ball in his left hand and lined up behind the pointed triangles on the floor.

We were at Jack & Jill Lanes, a bowling alley near my house, on an otherwise nondescript Saturday morning. Larry was the manager of the Village Green Trailer Court that his family owned and where my family lived. He was also a volunteer youth leader in our community. He had befriended me when I was seventeen by asking about my interests. I told him I liked to bowl.

"Well, let's go bowling then," he said.

It was obvious Larry had not spent much time in a bowling alley. He might have been an accomplished athlete (he was a professional tennis player and coached tennis at the local university), but he didn't know a five-step from a three-step. On one approach he dropped the ball behind him.

I had grown up around bowling alleys. My stepfather bowled in two leagues. My mother bowled. My brother bowled. Bowling was our family recreation of choice.

I at first assumed Larry was interested in bowling,

too. But what he was really interested in was helping me make good choices in my life. He took his youth leadership duties seriously; he was a friend to many youth in our area whom he took under his wing. He had watched me around the trailer court, a teenager going the typical hundred miles an hour without a thought about where he was headed next. He saw potential in me, and he wanted to help me see and realize that full potential.

He didn't invite me to the country club. He came to where the people on the west side of the tracks spent their time every Saturday. He came to my turf. He took off his tennis shoes and put on bowling shoes. After we bowled, we talked about all the possibilities and choices ahead for me. Larry Hall (no relation) became an important mentor in my life. I could see that this coach of athletes really cared about me. He would say, "Kevin, you can go down this path, or you can go down that path," and then we'd talk about what those choices meant and where they might lead. This young man—he wasn't much older than I was—helped guide me toward decisions that have positively impacted the rest of my life. He encouraged me to continue my schooling. He warned me to stay away from drugs and other addictions. Most of all, he was a great mentor and role model for selfless service. I don't think our relationship would ever have progressed if he hadn't first met me where I lived and taken the care to walk along my path.

The impact of his mentoring changed the course of my life.

Afternoons with Arthur

Today in our word study session I realized that Arthur loves dirty words.

Words that describe dirt are his favorites.

In earlier sessions he taught me words like "pathfinder," to describe a leader who gets down at ground level to identify for others where to hunt and travel, and "humility," a word derived from humus, the dark rich organic soil that promotes healthy growth and development.

Arthur explained that today's word, "empathy," is another that springs from the soil. "Pathy" comes from *path,* and "em" is *in.* Empathy is *walking the path of another.* If you don't get on another's path, if you don't go where he or she has gone, you can't truly understand what that person is experiencing.

He further pointed out that "communication," empathy's close cousin, is yet another word associated with dirt. "Communication" comes from the Latin "communicare," which means *to share in common.* To share in common requires coming together on common ground.

Arthur reminisced about visiting Italy with a group of students soon after he founded the study abroad program at the university. As they were traveling through the Italian countryside, their bus broke down, causing a long delay. It happened that they were near the village of Banubecco, a place Arthur knew well. It was where he was stationed during World War II when he helped decrypt German communications for the Allies.

When the bus was finally fixed, the students looked around for Arthur and could not find him. Concerned that they had lost their professor, they spread out and searched the village, where eventually they found "Arturo" speaking fluent Italian to a large crowd of enthralled Italians. He had no trouble passing the time while the bus was being repaired. With his language acumen and his knowledge of the people and the land, he and the villagers were indeed standing on common ground as he walked again along their path for this remarkable reunion.

BENEFITS VERSUS FEATURES

I have spent a good portion of my life in the professional sales field. I have been a salesman myself. I have trained and led a sales force and studied the methods of some of the world's highest-performing sales professionals. In the course of that I have come to realize that one of the key attributes of outstanding salespeople is the ability to anticipate the needs of others.

Average salespeople sell features. They talk about what this product or service does. Phenomenal sales professionals sell benefits. They talk about what the product or service can do for *you*. It's the difference between an ordinary car salesperson who explains that the ignition key includes a feature that unlocks the trunk and a master sales professional who explains that when you're walking to the car with your groceries in your arms, that trunk will rise so you don't have to set anything down. Customers don't buy features; they buy benefits. Master salespeople who understand how to walk the path of another are first and foremost great communicators.

THE ILLUSION OF COMMUNICATION

A restaurant owner in the Caribbean, tired of the humidity turning his sugar bowls into sugar balls, decided he would remedy the situation by ordering individual packets of sugar that his customers could open when they were ready to add sugar to their coffee and tea.

His instruction to the staff on the morning the packets arrived was simply this: take the old sugar out of the bowls, clean them, and replace it with the new sugar. Then the manager left.

While he was gone, his employees dutifully proceeded to open each individual packet of sugar and pour the contents into the newly cleaned sugar bowls. As they did so, they wondered aloud to one another, "Why in the world would he want us to do it like this?"

Who was responsible for the poor communication? Was it the sender or the receiver?

The answer, of course, is both.

George Bernard Shaw expressed it best when he quipped, "The problem with communication is the illusion that it has occurred."

As we establish common ground by truly *walking the path of others,* our ability to influence positive change is increased exponentially. When we fail to empathize, we invariably create the illusion that communication has occurred, when in fact it hasn't. Empathy on both sides would have prevented the misunderstanding—empathy from the owner (what are they hearing?) and empathy from the employees (what is he thinking?).

NEVER ASSUME ANYTHING

It's remarkable just how much can go wrong when the all-important ingredients of empathy and common ground aren't firmly established.

For me, the point was driven home all too hard when I was a senior in high school and put in charge of the annual fall homecoming celebration.

I had read about a school in New York that had staged a Volkswagen race down the football field and decided that would be a good activity to hold at halftime of our homecoming football game. The plan was to have each class—sophomores, juniors, and seniors—push a Volkswagen Bug from one end of the field to the other. First Volkswagen to the end zone was the winner. I envisioned the esprit de corps, the fun, the excitement that such an unusual event would generate. With the other student body officers, I presented the idea to Mr. Oyler, our faculty advisor. Mr. Oyler was no pushover. He'd been an All-American football player in college and was constantly trying to teach us to be better communicators and better leaders, while also giving us plenty of room to figure out things for ourselves.

I remember the day I came out of his office, having sold him on the Volkswagen race. I assured him that the execution would be flawless. I told him that we would cover the new track so it wouldn't be damaged as the Volkswagens rolled across it to the football field. Other precautions would be put in place, and all our lofty expectations would be met. Although it was something that had never been tried before at our high school, I assured one and all that it was something that we would be able to talk about for a long time to come. Unfortunately, that proved to be the case.

I still remember walking to the field at halftime of the football game, taking the microphone, and saying, "We will now start our Volkswagen race!" It was like a mob scene after that. People ran out of the stands and started pushing the cars. I didn't have a chance to explain the rules or even have time to say, "Go." The sophomores had no driver for their car. Within a matter of seconds they veered into the juniors' lane and crashed into their Volkswagen, T-boning the side. The juniors responded by jumping on the sophomores' car and smashing in the roof. None of the three cars made it to the end zone before Mr. Oyler made his way to the middle of the football field, microphone in hand, and said, "Would Kevin Hall please report to my office."

I walked the thousand or so painful steps from the football field to his office, with the rest of the student body officers following behind, thankful they weren't me. When we opened the door, Mr. Oyler had written three words on the chalkboard:

Never Assume Anything.

Mr. Oyler reminded me of our earlier conversation when I assured him of a flawless event. He reviewed all the things I should have thought through but didn't. He asked if I'd assumed that I could clearly communicate the directions of the race before chaos erupted. Did I assume that sophomores who didn't have driver's licenses would have a driver in their Volkswagen? Did I assume the cars would all go in a straight line? Did I assume the cars would all be insured? (Only one was.)

My big opportunity to show what kind of leader and communicator I was had come and gone, and I sure hadn't nailed it. All I could think of was a line from the Paul Newman movie *Cool Hand Luke,* "What we have here is a failure to communicate." But it was memorable. I can't tell you how many people came up to me the rest of the year and said, "Wow, that was really something, Kevin. We'll never forget that night."

COMMANDER'S INTENT

So much that can go wrong, and right, in communication rests on both sender and receiver knowing the intent of the message. When you know the *why,* you know the *way.*

In the case of the Caribbean restaurant with the soggy sugar problem, if the owner had clearly communicated to his staff that their intent was to run a first-rate restaurant that always thought of its customers' needs first, the staffers would have been able to know not to tear open those individual sugar packets even if the orders had been muddled or murky. In *Made to Stick,* authors Dan and Chip Heath write about a phrase used in the army, "commander's intent." It speaks to the real meaning and purpose of a commander's communication. The wording of the order isn't what's important; what's important is to comprehend what the commander intended by the order.

The word "comprehend" comes from "com," meaning *together,* and "prehender," *to grasp.* "Comprehend" is *to grasp together.*

When leaders invest the time to make sure both parties comprehend, misunderstandings disappear.

Norman Brinker, the legendary business executive referred to in Chapter 6, was renowned for success in his industry, and as you talk to anyone who worked with him or was mentored by him, the common response is that he was a rare and effective communicator.

His leadership style included four absolutes: (1) When he had meetings with team members, he went to their offices, instead of requiring that they come to him. (2) He asked the questions, and they provided the answers. (3) He made sure they did the majority of the talking. (4) He expressed gratitude and appreciation frequently. (At his memorial service, Doug Brooks, the current CEO of Brinker International, recalled how Norman had sent him fifty-three personal thank-you notes and letters of appreciation and how he had saved and cherished every one of them.) With this kind of empathic communication, he consistently produced executives who moved on to top positions in the industry. In fact, over twenty former team members now run publicly traded companies.

UNDERSTANDING CLEARLY

In his groundbreaking book *The Four Agreements*, Don Miguel Ruiz writes about the importance of clear, open, two-way communication. In elaborating on his Third Agreement, Don't Make Assumptions, he advises, "Find the courage to ask questions and to express what you really want. Communicate with others as clearly as you can to avoid misunderstanding, sadness, and drama.

With just this one agreement you can completely transform your life."

Stephen R. Covey has taught me on numerous occasions that "nothing is more validating and affirming than feeling understood. And the moment a person begins feeling understood, that person becomes far more open to influence and change. Empathy is to the heart what air is to the body."

Unfortunately, in our day and age, it is a luxury to be understood.

In pure etymology, "understand" means to *stand among*. It doesn't mean to stand beneath or below. It means to stand *with*.

True pathfinders lead from common ground. They are on the path, eyeball to eyeball, elbow to elbow, shoulder to shoulder with their followers. They are guide-and-show leaders.

We Can Always Talk

Some of the best parenting advice I ever received came from a woman I once worked with at Franklin, Patricia Murray. Pat was a former Miss Hawaii and runner-up to Miss America, but what impressed me most about her was the relationship she and her husband, Harry, had with their children. They talked all the time, about everything and anything. Clearly, there was a high degree of love and trust among them. I asked Pat how they had managed to develop such a great relationship. She said that early on she and Harry established two rules with their children. The first was that they could always be friends, no matter what. The second was that they could always talk, no matter what.

"Those two principles have seen us through every challenge," she said.

Sherry and I were just starting our family at the time, and we took her advice to heart. We established the same rules in our home with our children. This spirit of wide-open communication—no matter what—made goal setting a natural progression in our family. Each year we would sit down with our children and help them identify their goals and dreams. They couldn't be our goals, they needed to be their goals. Our children needed dreams that called to them. These "interviews" produced a pattern of communication that led to far-reaching, positive results and allowed us to guide and lead our children in their various paths.

THE VALUE OF WORDS

It's easy to take words for granted. But when a person's brain starts to slip away, as happens when someone is caught in the clutches of Alzheimer's disease, every single word becomes so much more valuable.

I have a neighbor and friend, Jim Dyer, whose wife and soul mate, Renie, was stricken with Alzheimer's. Two years into her disease, as her ability to remember and communicate diminished, Jim knew the time was rapidly approaching when she wouldn't be sharing any words with him or anyone else. He began listening more intently and taking notes of what she said. Every word became a treasure. Over a five-year period he accumulated more than

8,000 of those words and recorded and catalogued them in a journal. Week by week, her word count dropped. As time progressed, Renie seldom spoke at all. It was as if she limited herself to only that which was most important.

On occasion, she would speak in a language Jim couldn't quite decipher. But he noticed that by just saying the words and knowing that someone was listening had a calming, satisfying effect on Renie.

On Thanksgiving, surrounded by family and friends, Renie hadn't said a word all day. She used to love playing the piano, and her son Steve wheeled her over close to the piano while her grandson Robbie played. As he concluded, everyone in the room heard Renie say two words in loud, clear English—the two most important words she could have said on that day—"Thank you."

We should never underestimate or take for granted the power of communication. We should never underestimate the power of the right word spoken at the right time. Words connect us to each other. They make up what we hear and what we say. They are the essence of who we collectively are.

EMPATHY AND SUFFERING

Speaking of empathy, Og Mandino writes, "With love I will tear down the wall of suspicion and hate which they have built round their hearts and in its place I will build bridges so that my love may enter their souls." A close friend and coaching client, Dave Blanchard, CEO of the Og Mandino Group, continues, "Our character has been forged in the furnace of adversity. We know what pain feels like. We cannot change the past. However, we can choose to use these reference points as a rich resource to assist us in better understanding and connecting with people. When we use our life experiences in the service of others, we will finally find purpose in our suffering, joy in our journey and much needed healing in our souls."

MY JOURNAL THOUGHTS ON *Empathy*

To be a leader and true pathfinder, I need to discover that which sustains life through active listening and astute observation.

Empathy means walking the path of another.

Listening has the power to take me to another level of human mastery and an elite level of leadership.

Ernest Hemingway said, "I have learned a great deal from listening carefully. Most people never listen."

What are the characteristics of empathic listeners?

What do they do when communicating?

What do other people do differently as a result of me being in their midst?

How can I listen more empathically?

In every encounter I can choose to exhibit understanding and empathy, or I can choose to be critical and judgmental. The first choice leads to meaningful relationships; the second leads to a life of empty assumptions and frustration.

I choose to tap into my unlimited capacity to empathize and feel for others, for a purpose-filled path is not meant to be traveled alone.

IDENTIFY AND HONOR AN EXAMPLE OF
Empathy

SELECT someone you know who personifies Empathy.

WRITE that person's name in the box provided below.

REACH OUT to and teach that person the meaning of "Empathy" and explain why he or she personifies this word.

CHAPTER NINE

Coach

Help thy brother's boat across and lo!
thine own has reached the shore.

— Hindu Proverb —

In old Hungary, along the Danube River between Budapest and Vienna, there was a village by the name of Kocs that produced the world's finest horse-drawn vehicles. Skilled wheelwrights fashioned these conveyances with spring suspension to comfortably carry royalty over the bumpy river road that connected the two great cities. These carriages borrowed their name from the small township where they were skillfully designed and came to be known as "coaches."

Originally crafted for aristocracy, coaches carried important people to their desired destinations in luxury and ease. Their compact, sturdy, and elegant design far surpassed any mode of transportation that had come before, and coaches soon became the rage of fifteenth-century Europe.

Over time, other forms of transportation adopted the term "coach." Passengers traveled the far reaches of the western frontier of America by stagecoach and railway coach. In Europe a motor coach became synonymous with a luxury car or travel bus.

But however far-reaching and prevalent the word has become since the first coach rolled out of production in

Kocs, the meaning has not changed. A "coach" remains something, or someone, who *carries a valued person from where they are to where they want to be.*

A COACH BY ANY OTHER NAME

In other cultures and languages, coaches are known by many different names and titles.

In Japan, a "sensei" is *one who has gone farther down the path.* In martial arts, it is the designation for master.

In Sanskrit, a "guru" is *one with great knowledge and wisdom.* "Gu" means *darkness,* and "ru" means *light*—a guru takes someone from the darkness into the light.

In Tibet, a "lama" is *one with spirituality and authority to teach.* In Tibetan Buddhism, the Dalai Lama is the highest-ranking teacher.

In Italy, a "maestro" is *a master teacher of music.* It is short for "maestro di cappella," meaning *master of the chapel.*

In France, a "tutor" is a *private teacher.* The term dates to the fourteenth century and refers to one who served as a watchman.

In England, a "guide" is one *who knows and shows the way.* It denotes the ability to see and point out the better course.

In Greece, a "mentor" is *a wise and trusted advisor.* In *The Odyssey,* Homer's Mentor was a protective and supportive counselor.

All these words describe the same role: *one who goes before and shows the way.* Coaches point out the sharp turns, potholes, perils, and pitfalls of the road being traveled. They steer clear of dead-end streets and unnecessary detours as they safely navigate us to our desired destinations. Whether they are leading or teaching or showing or guiding or mentoring, they are coaches. And they are indispensable in helping us find our path and purpose.

Afternoons with Arthur

Arthur's eyes sparkled when I settled into his comfortable room and talked of the coaches from Kocs. He was delighted to affirm my story about the origin of the word "coach." He informed me that he had in fact traveled the very road along the Danube River between Vienna and Budapest that ran through the village of Kocs. The memory obviously pleased him. But what pleased him even more was the fact that I had been doing some homework on my own.

I noticed a special enthusiasm in Arthur when others demonstrated a love for words that approached his own. I observed extra energy when he conducted his "Culture Capsule" lectures, and someone in the audience would become animated about the word they were discussing that day. Arthur's face would light up, and his large hands would motion excitedly as he plunged into the conversation. I saw the same energy on the many occasions when I was with him in his room, and one member or another of his family would call on the phone, and just like that Arthur was talking to a son or daughter in Italian or German or some other language I could not understand. It clearly delighted him when others took pleasure in words and language.

As we talked about the village of Kocs, Arthur kept me spellbound with a memory he had from the 1930s of standing with a crowd in a public square in Vienna listening to a man deliver a speech. The speaker was the chancellor of Germany, Adolf Hitler. Before he spewed his politics of hate across Europe and started World War II, Arthur heard firsthand the enormous power in Hitler's voice. He remembered his ability to incite the crowd with nothing more than his choice of words and the inflection he used to deliver them. Words, Arthur reminded me, can bring about much that is positive, or much that is destructive.

THE VALUE OF COACHING

It can be most useful to take inventory of the many coaches in our lives and make note of how they keep us on path and purpose. Throughout this book I mention and pay tribute to many people who have filled this crucial role in my life. These coaches go by different names and titles—teacher, guide, mentor, mother, friend, professor, to name a few. But in one way or another, all have carried me to places I never could have gone on my own.

Recognizing the value of a coach can be the first step toward improved performance. But it isn't always easy. Even in the world of sports, where coaches are ubiquitous, a coach's importance can sometimes be undervalued and overlooked.

In the sport of bicycle racing, which is a personal

passion of mine, a revolution of sorts took place when Lance Armstrong started using coaches in ways they'd never been used before. After recovering from cancer, Armstrong used nutritionists to make sure his immune system was functioning at its optimal level. He didn't stop there. He sought out experts to fit his bicycle and his equipment. He consulted designers to determine the type of custom clothing he would wear in a time trial to better cut through the wind. In a sport that seemed as simple as turning pedals on a bike—something most of us mastered in childhood—he brought in coaches who measured how much power was being produced by each pedal stroke.

He also brought coaches into the bike races themselves. It had long been tradition that once a race started, the cyclists were on their own, left to rely on their wits and instincts. But beyond using coaches to help him prepare for the race, Lance maintained constant radio contact with his coaches so they could advise him during the race. Carrying it yet another step further, once the race was finished, Lance brought in a food coach, a chef to prepare the kinds of meals that would help him recover as quickly and efficiently as possible from the exertion of the day. When it comes to learning from the best in the world, Lance Armstrong left no stone unturned. "Team Lance," they called it, and bicycle racing had never seen anything like it.

I saw "Team Lance" firsthand when I traveled with some cycling friends to France to watch the Tour de France. We were at an outdoor café in Evian on the shores of beautiful Lake Geneva, awaiting the start of that day's stage race, when we were joined by Lance's trainer and performance coach, Chris Carmichael.

We asked Chris how Lance had been able to take his gifts and talents and become the most dominant rider in the world. He explained that a lot of Lance's success could be attributed to his willingness to change the cadence of his pedal strokes. Most cyclists turned their pedals at an average rate of between 70 and 80 revolutions per minute. Not Lance. He increased his tempo until he was averaging between 90 and 100 revolutions, even when he was climbing hills. Carmichael had suggested to Lance that he go to the almost unheard-of higher cadence to take advantage of his lean, compact muscles. By "spinning" in higher gears, he could capitalize on his unique physiology.

"Just watch how he keeps getting stronger," Carmichael said. This was early in the Tour de France. Several days later, when the race concluded in Paris, Lance Armstrong, just as his coach had predicted, rode down the Champs-Elysées wearing the coveted yellow jersey signifying his victory. As we watched him mount the winner's podium, I could imagine a very satisfied Coach Carmichael standing nearby.

Lance Armstrong, one of the most successful athletes in history, exemplifies the importance of not just surrounding himself with coaches, but being eminently coachable.

Having a coach is one thing; listening to that coach is another.

A COACH FOR ALL REASONS

No one I know of in the business world recognizes the value of coaches more than Harvey Mackay, bestselling author, internationally renowned speaker, and founder and chairman of Mackay Envelope Company. Harvey recently told me that he has a coach for almost every area of his life. He has a speaking coach. He has a writing coach. He has a business coach. He has a financial coach. He has a life coach. He has a tennis coach. He has a running coach. He has a golf coach. He even has a Ping-Pong coach. In all, he has more than a dozen personal coaches. And why? Because he's realized how much more he can accomplish through the aid of good coaching. He understands how invaluable it is to go to someone who is at the very top of the learning curve and be tutored by them. It's helped him succeed in business, it's helped him succeed as an athlete, and it's helped him develop into one of the world's most sought-after writers and speakers. Coaches have enriched all the areas of his life that are meaningful to him.

COACHES SEE POTENTIAL

Among all the different kinds and types of coaches, the common thread is that they are all teachers. To "teach" means *to show*. Teachers don't just tell; they illustrate, they model, they show.

Marva Collins is considered one of the world's greatest teachers. She started the Westside Preparatory School inside her own home in an impoverished neighborhood in Chicago. She opened the doors to students who had been abandoned and left behind by the public school system. These were students labeled "learning disabled." They were failing. They had trouble reading and spelling. They were considered unteachable and uncoachable—until Marva took them in and *showed* them a better way.

This visionary teacher would not accept social stereotypes. She would not accept mediocrity. She would not accept excuses. She believed that "there is a brilliant child locked inside every student." Marva told her students they had a choice. They could take the path of not learning, of illiteracy, and wind up with a dead-end job, unable to provide for their needs. Or they could choose to become educated and open unforeseen horizons for themselves and for those they cared for.

She forsook busy work and rote memorization, replacing it with active participation and a demand that the students practice self-discipline. She believed that a teacher should make learning contagious and create an environment in which one idea sparks another.

Marva was able to take children who had been told they were illiterate and help them become fluent in language. They were able to read from the greatest writers—Plato, Socrates, Homer. "Throwaway" students began quoting Shakespeare. Eventually, and with a lot of hard work, graduates of Westside Prep were accepted at Harvard, Princeton, Columbia, Oxford, Yale, and Stanford.

Her remarkable story was featured on *60 Minutes*. Two presidents, George H. W. Bush and Bill Clinton, asked her to become secretary of education, but she turned them down in favor of teaching one student at a time.

My wife, Sherry, and I had the privilege of spending three days with Marva and her husband, Franklin, also a teacher, at their beautiful home in Hilton Head, South Carolina.

In her expansive library, Marva talked about teaching being the key that got everything started. "I have discovered few learning disabled students in my three decades of teaching," she said. "I have, however, discovered many, many victims of teaching inabilities."

She believed that a good teacher should make a poor student good, and a good student superior. I remember her saying, "When our students fail, we, as teachers, have also failed."

She focused on identifying and magnifying each student's unique gifts. Her mantra to her students was "Trust yourself. Think for yourself. Act for yourself. Speak for yourself. Be yourself."

She embodied the philosophy "You can't teach what you don't know, and you can't guide where you don't go."

We don't have to teach thousands, hundreds, or even dozens. If we can show one person the way, if we can bring one person from darkness into light, if we can make a difference in one person's development, we have succeeded as a teacher and a coach. It is true that when you light someone else's path, you see your own more clearly.

I have found this to be true in my own coaching experiences. On a weekly basis I have the privilege of coaching top performers in business, sales, athletics, speaking, and writing. I often receive as much or more from them as they receive from me.

Jim Newman, an early mentor who was instrumental in my involvement in Viktor Frankl's envisioned Statue of Responsibility, had a saying that he would often share with me. "Kevin, if you want happiness, if you want peace, if you want fulfillment in life, rejoice in the success of others." What a model. What a goal. What a target for anyone who wants to be a coach. Is there anything more rewarding than watching someone you care about, someone you've worked and planned with, reach and accomplish things that person never dreamed possible?

REACHING OUT TO EVERYONE

When our oldest son, Colby, was a junior in high school, we moved to California. He was an avid soccer player and understandably anxious about how the move would affect his developing soccer career, particularly since he would be enrolling in one of the largest high schools in the state, one that had a reputation for producing outstanding soccer players.

Shortly after we unloaded the moving trucks, I drove Colby to the high school soccer field, where the boys' soccer team was practicing. We stepped out to watch for a minute, and I noticed a boy warming up who had obvious disabilities. He could not walk normally, let alone run. As he chased the ball, he didn't run so much as shuffle. Later, I found he suffered from cerebral palsy.

Another parent was standing nearby. I asked him if the disabled boy was one of the team managers. "No," came the reply. "He's on the team. Coach Skaff wants him to play."

That was all I needed to hear about Coach Don Skaff. I knew then that Colby had come to a solid program.

During the season, I watched Coach Skaff include the boy, whose name was Sean, in every drill, every practice, and every game. He wasn't a starter, and he didn't play regularly. The coach did not lose sight of his responsibility to the school and the other players to field a competitive team. (They won the league championship that year.) He also did not lose sight of his responsibility to be compassionate and inclusive. In practices and sometimes in games, he found a time and place for Sean, who beamed like Beckham every time he got on the field.

As the season progressed, the coach's actions had a positive effect on the rest of the players. Rather than resent Sean, whose body was not quite as complete and whole as their own, they emulated their coach and went out of their way to accept and encourage him. I'm convinced it made them a more cohesive team.

After the season, I talked to Coach Skaff about his reasons for including Sean on the team. He told me that it had as much to do with what Sean could bring to the team as what the team could bring to Sean. He sensed Sean's desire, his spirit and attitude and positivity, in the face of, and in spite of, his physical disabilities. "Sean never said, 'I can't do it,'" said the coach. "It was amazing how serious he was to make the team, how hard he worked, harder than anybody else. He brought so much to the table. The other players respected him and in turn realized how truly fortunate they were. It made them all work a little harder. It brought us together."

This perceptive coach had a plan and it worked—for *everyone*.

VALIDATION IS POWER

I had an opportunity to get to know Meg Whitman when we worked together on a presidential candidate's campaign. Meg is legendary as an innovator and motivator. She took over a small Internet business with a handful of employees and turned it into a $16 billion company with thousands of employees and millions of customers called eBay.

Meg built eBay on the strength of one word. "My favorite word of all words," she calls it. That word is "validation."

"Validate" comes from the Latin "valere," which means *to be strong*. In the eyes of the law, "valid" means to be *legally acceptable*. When you are validated, you are given strength, power, and authority.

At eBay, Meg created a unique, timely feedback system that constantly and effectively assured customers and employees alike that they were in charge of their transactions, that they had power. Every transaction by buyer and seller was instantly rated, resulting in an overall feedback or trust score. This confidence-building validation became the backbone for a virtual marketplace that was embraced around the world.

Said Meg, "When you give people validation, it gives them power, it enables them to do remarkable things. It's what makes the world go round."

Effective coaching emphasizes strengths and abilities, not weaknesses and disabilities.

A LEADER MUST LEARN TO FOLLOW

At its core, coaching is reciprocal. It is never a one-way street. Astute coaches learn from those they are coaching.

Jon Luther, formerly the CEO and currently the executive chairman of the board of the multibillion-dollar conglomerate Dunkin' Brands, likes to tell the story about his first job as a manager in the hospitality industry. He had just graduated from college and had made enough of an impression with his new company, Service Systems, that they sent him to run the food operation at Canisius College in his hometown of Buffalo, New York.

"I was twenty-four years old," remembered Jon. "I walked in with my Princeton tie and my button-down shirt, and I was absolutely lost. I looked over, and there was this wonderful older woman, Sarah, who was the line cook. 'Kid, you don't know what's going on, do you?' she said. 'Come on, I'll show you the way.'

"She became my mentor. She taught me the back of the house. She showed me everything I was supposed to know but didn't know. She saved me. I learned that no person is inconsequential and that every job matters."

Years passed. Jon moved on in his career and eventually was named vice president of Aramark Services, a large national food services company that goes by the initials ARA. His appointment was written up in the Buffalo newspaper, a one-by-two-inch article with a small photograph under the headline "Local Boy Makes Good."

Not long after that, Jon was sitting in his office in Philadelphia when the phone rang. An ARA associate named Tom Lawless was on the line, calling from Buffalo.

"Hey, Jon," he said. "Aramark just picked up the Canisius College account, and I've been interviewing the employees about transfers. I met with a woman named Sarah Henley. When we sat down, she said, 'ARA. Isn't that the company Jon Luther works for?' I told her it was, and she reached into her purse and pulled out this little newspaper article with your picture, pointed to it, and said, 'Taught him everything he knows.'"

"Tell her she's right," answered Jon.

"To be a leader, you must first learn to follow" is Jon Luther's advice when he talks about leadership. "And never underestimate the power of a relationship. I have learned that you can never forget those who have helped you along the way."

MY JOURNAL THOUGHTS ON *Coach*

When I teach a skill to another, I learn it twice myself.

Acquiring knowledge and experience brings its own reward.

Sharing knowledge and experience with others brings an exponentially larger set of rewards.

Remember the Asian expression "He makes things easier for himself who makes things easier for others."

The word "expert" comes from the Latin "experiri" and means one who helps you try something new.

Experts help shorten the "learning curve" for those they guide down the path.

Authentic coaches focus on the performance of those they coach.

I commit to reaching out and passing along whatever skills and talents I have acquired to others. In so doing, I gain a sense of contribution and contentment that cannot be achieved in any other way.

Deepak Chopra describes it like this:
"Everyone has a purpose in life . . . a unique gift or special talent to give to others. And when we blend this unique talent with service to others, we experience the ecstasy and exultation of our own spirit, which is the ultimate goal of all goals."

I can't carry others to their desired destination without getting closer to my own.

IDENTIFY AND HONOR AN OUTSTANDING
Coach

SELECT someone you know whose behavior best reflects the principles of a Coach.

WRITE that person's name in the box provided below.

REACH OUT to and teach that person the meaning of "Coach" and explain why he or she personifies this word.

CHAPTER TEN

―――⁓―――

Ollín

It is not light that we need but fire;
it is not the gentle shower, but thunder.
We need the storm,
the whirlwind, and the earthquake.

— FREDERICK DOUGLASS —

When an earthquake or great storm shook the earth, the ancient Aztecs described such power with a single word:

"Ollin."

It is a word that can be found on the Aztec calendar and on many of the instruments used in sacred pre-Columbian ceremonies. Pronounced ALL-in, it is an expression of immense depth that conveys intense and immediate movement. Stemming from the ancient Nahuatl language, "Ollin" is derived from "yollotl," meaning *heart,* and "yolistli," meaning *life.* "Ollin" means *to move and act now with all your heart.* It means to follow your path in life wholeheartedly. To experience Ollin, we have to get "All in."

When an earthquake occurs, it signals it's now time to move and act with full purpose of heart.

The Aztecs envisioned wearing your heart on your face to allow your eyes to open and see more clearly. When we view our path with clarity, we move with accelerated purpose and intent. We go forward with a full and committed heart. The Aztecs called it an Ollin heart. They believed that everyone had a sacred path that led to theirs life's purpose. It was up to individual to discover what they needed to do in their life and then give it their all. They believed that if everyone could find their purpose, the thing that made their hearts beat fast, the entire society could find its Ollin. It was not just an individual endeavor. It was a communal endeavor.

Ollin confirms that words are sacred and have the power to inspire us to change the world for the better.

Other cultures have similar words to describe the concept of committed action and being "All in." Kenton Worthington, a coaching client of mine and one of the top network marketers in the world, taught me that Hungarians have a similar word, "Egyensuly" (pronounced edge-en-SHOE-ee). It means *one-weighted focus*. It calls for putting all your weight behind what you are doing, and if you don't, you run the risk of falling into the pitfalls associated with indecision and inaction. Being half-hearted, uncommitted, the very opposite of Ollin, carries with it its own penalties.

Afternoons with Arthur

Every once in a while, during our study sessions, I would engage Arthur in a game I called "Stump the Professor." The rules were simple enough. I would throw out a word. If Arthur couldn't identify its origin, he was stumped.

For over three years I was unsuccessful, until the day I brought up the word "Ollin."

Arthur stared at me with his mouth open, a rare blank look on his face.

"It's an Aztec word," I explained. "It means going 'All in.'"

"Well," he said, a wide smile spreading across his face. "You sure stumped me on that one!"

Our discussion soon moved to what it means to go "All in." Arthur quickly recovered by connecting the phrase to "opportunity." He explained that the root word of opportunity is *port,* meaning the entryway by water into a city or place of business. In earlier days, when the tide and winds were right and the port opened, it allowed entry to do commerce, to visit, or to invade and conquer. But only those who recognized the opening could take advantage of the *open port.*

You couldn't truly go "All in," he wisely pointed out, without first recognizing and taking advantage of the opportunity that preceded it. This type of action isn't stagnant. It isn't stationary. It is about moving forward with commitment and resolve. "Resolve" comes from the Latin "resolvere," and means *to loosen.* We usually use the term "solvent" to describe a liquid that loosens and releases one or more other substances. That is what resolve—true resolve—accomplishes in our lives. It shakes loose what may be hindering our progress.

Acting with purpose loosens the shackles of procrastination. "Procrastination" comes from the Latin "pro," meaning *forward,* and "crastinus," signifying *tomorrow.* This corrosive form of inactivity deceives many into believing that they will somehow move *forward tomorrow.*

Progress is made one step at a time. "Pro" means *forward,* and "gress" is *to move.* When we make "progress" in life, we *move forward* on our journey.

Then Arthur, whose "Stump the Professor" winning streak had just come to an end, winked at me as he said, "Kevin, you're really starting to progress with your linguistic prowess."

TOTAL COMMITMENT

I once jumped out of a perfectly safe airplane. I went to the Economy Jumping School, where for $45 and after four hours of training you earn the right to fly 3,000 feet above the earth in a Cessna 172 without a door . . . and jump.

I took three friends with me, and when the plane got in position, the four of us were huddled as far away from that open door as possible. The pilot was in the left seat, and the jumpmaster was crouched in front of the opening, ready to call our names. When my appointed time came, the jumpmaster said, "Kevin, it's time to jump," and I shoved my friend, whose name is also Kevin, forward. The jumpmaster pointed at me and shouted, "No, you, with the little, round face!"

It's at this moment, when you slide over to the opening and peek out at brown and green patches of ground far below, that you realize for the first time they don't stop the plane so you can jump. You're going seventy miles an hour, and they tell you to put both feet on this metal plate about the size of a shoe. Then you're supposed to lunge forward and hold onto the wing strut. About four feet out on the wing strut is a black line. You're told to make sure you shinny out past that black line because if you don't, you risk the chance of hitting the tail, and we all know bad things happen when you hit the tail.

So there I was, hanging on to the wing strut with my feet dangling beneath me. And I heard my jumpmaster scream the one-word command: "Jump!"

In training we were taught that when he said "Jump," we were supposed to immediately release and let go of the wing strut, arch our backs, and start counting, "Arch one thousand . . . arch two thousand . . . arch three thousand . . . arch four thousand . . . ," and by the time we got to "Arch five thousand," our parachute should open by the static line attached to the airplane.

But when the jumpmaster said, "Jump!" I had a hard time letting go. In fact, for a moment I pictured them landing the airplane with me hanging on to the edge of the wing.

Sensing my hesitation, my jumpmaster reached for a long wooden stick with a rubber hammer on the end of it. We had been warned beforehand that if we froze up and were not willing to jump, he would accommodate us by knocking our hand off the wing strut. As I saw him reach for the wooden stick, I let go of the wing. I forgot to count. Instead of saying, "Arch one thousand," I just went "Ahhhhgggaaaahhgggggg!"

It's at that point, after you've let go and you're totally committed to what you came for, that the rush, the fear, and the excitement all morph into one emotion. It's a truly exhilarating experience. Then, just seconds after that, if you're lucky, your chute opens, and mine did. All of a sudden it's all worth it. You're floating in air, gazing down at an earth that never looked more beautiful. You see the field you're supposed to land in; you see the windsock to help you gauge your angle of descent. Everything is in full color and sharp focus. You see the toggles on the parachute that help you turn. I did some 360s, then I was able to glide in and safely land. Moments later, the Cessna came in for its landing. If I'd never let go of the wing strut, the flight would have been significantly different for both me and the plane, and not in a good way.

PURPOSEFUL ACTION

Putting off today what we can do tomorrow runs contrary to nature. As Germany's greatest man of letters, Johann Wolfgang von Goethe, penned: "Nature knows no pause in progress and development, and attaches her curse on all inaction."

In *The Greatest Salesman in the World,* Og Mandino introduces an ancient scroll entitled "I will act now." It reads in part: "My procrastination which has held me back was born of fear and now I recognize this secret mined from the depths of all courageous hearts. Now I know that to conquer fear I must always act without hesitation and the flutters in my heart will vanish. Now I know that action reduces the lion of terror to an ant of equanimity."

FEAR is often nothing more than False Emotions Appearing Real. "Fear of failure" and "fear of success" can each be overcome by firmly placing one foot after another with unswerving position and steadfast resolution.

Purposeful action will always prevail over passive inaction. Confucius, the great Chinese philosopher, said, "Wherever you go, go with all your heart."

GIVING YOUR ALL

The philosophy of going "All in" can be especially curative when it comes to defining personal success. If "Ollin" is the measure, "winning" is possible no matter what the final outcome.

World-class runner Henry Marsh was the overwhelming favorite to win a gold medal in the 1984 Olympics in his specialty, the 3,000-meter steeplechase. It was almost a foregone conclusion that he would stand on the top step of the winner's podium, until he contracted a debilitating virus just days before his race.

The illness had him flat in bed, and he couldn't risk taking even the mildest of medications for fear of ingesting something on the list of banned drugs for Olympic athletes. Bed rest is hardly the preferred way to warm up for the biggest race of your career.

For most of his life, Henry had trained for this moment. He was thirty years old, at his peak as an athlete. He was ranked first in the world in the steeplechase, an event nearly two miles in length that includes a number of barriers, hurdles, and water jumps in a race that covers seven and a half laps around the track. At the American trials, the qualifying meet for the Olympics, he had finished first, winning the U.S. championship for the seventh year in a row. If anyone was poised to crown his career with an Olympic championship, it was Henry Marsh.

But then, at the worst possible time, he got sick. Through sheer force of will he got out of bed in time to make it through two qualifying races. In the Olympic final, after staying in contention through seven laps, he started to fade down the stretch. First a runner from Kenya pulled away from him, then a runner from France passed him, and finally, just a few inches from the finish line, his American teammate passed him. Henry finished fourth, one place out of the medals, and as soon as he crossed the finish line, he collapsed onto the track, unconscious, unable to move. Paramedics were called in to carry him from the track. It took him a half hour to recover and stand up again.

I met Henry a few months after all this happened, working together at Franklin. Around the office, he had a well-deserved reputation for being extremely positive. His optimism was contagious. We became close friends, and soon our kids called him "Uncle Henry." I have fond personal memories of joint business trips, shared family vacations, and lunchtime workouts. He was the uncle you always wanted around because of his penchant for looking on the bright side of things. When I heard in detail what happened to him at the Olympics, I asked him the obvious question: how was he able to stay positive after such a devastating disappointment?

In response to my question, he told me the rest of the story. He explained that he had a talk with himself before the final and promised that if he gave the race everything he had, if he could look himself in the mirror and truthfully admit that he hadn't held anything back, then he wouldn't be hard on himself no matter where he placed. He'd gotten sick, but he couldn't do anything about that. All he asked of himself was his complete commitment.

"I was satisfied I gave it my all," said the man who collapsed an inch beyond the finish line.

So he refused to beat himself up and declined to join the chorus of well-meaning people who attempted to console him (he received thousands of sympathy cards and letters after the event) for what they saw as colossal bad luck. But to Henry it was a triumph, no matter what the scoreboard said. He had entered a race and given it everything he could give. He had practiced Ollin. He refused to focus on what some saw as a loss. He saw it as a personal victory.

That attitude prevailed in his athletic accomplishments the next season, when Henry won yet another American steeplechase championship, finishing ahead of, among others, the teammate who had finished ahead of him for the bronze medal at the Olympics. After what some viewed as his "greatest disappointment," he had his best year ever as a runner, achieving a personal goal of running a sub-four-minute mile and setting a new national record in the steeplechase that wouldn't be broken for more than twenty years. His positive attitude and habit of giving his all have carried him to success in the business world, where he excels as a trainer, speaker, and network-marketing entrepreneur.

It's the private victories that matter most and are felt the deepest and last the longest. It's the internal triumphs that aren't recorded on scoreboards or broadcast on the eleven o'clock news that define who we are. Ollin is what determines success in our lives, instead of the conventional measure of winning and losing. With that as a definition of success, it is possible for everyone to win all the time.

DON'T BACK IN

Have you ever seen a surfer get out of his car and casually walk to the waves? When I'm in San Clemente, California, home to some of the world's best surf spots, I find it entertaining to watch surfers heading for the beach. They don't walk. They don't trot. They run. They leap. They bound. Why? The reason seems obvious: they can't wait to get out there—to get "All in." There is nothing about the way they approach the ocean that suggests indecision or ambivalence. They don't back in. They don't approach the water gingerly and dip their toe in. They are the picture of enthusiasm and total commitment. They personify Ollin.

EXPANDING OUR COMFORT ZONES

An early mentor of mine, Jim Newman, author of *Release Your Brakes!* and one of the early pioneers in the area of human development and potential—a man who worked with and influenced such noted thought leaders as Denis Waitley, Brian Tracy, Stephen R. Covey, Lou Tice, and Jack Canfield—taught about the importance of letting go of the seemingly safe and secure so we can truly soar. He called the places we gravitate to and try to hang on to "comfort zones."

We all have comfort zones. We have comfort clothes, comfort friends, comfort food. Whose food do you eat at a potluck dinner? Probably your own. And why do you do that? Because you know the hands that prepared it, you know how it tastes, and you know it's safe. We wear comfort clothes because they're soft and comfortable. When I mow my lawn, I wear the clothes I picked up in Hawaii twenty years ago. They're not in style, they're full of holes, but I am one happy camper out there mowing my lawn because they feel so comforting and familiar. We find friends who make us feel safe and secure, and we are content to stick with them, shying away from taking the risks required to form new friendships.

But as Jim Newman taught, much of what we want and seek in life that is meaningful and significant is just beyond the edge of our comfort zone. If we're not willing to venture "out there," we will never find and have all that we truly desire. We will never fulfill our complete purpose. To reach our goals and dreams, to experience life in full color, to soar to dreamed-of and hoped-for heights, we have to expand our comfort zone. We have to be willing to do what is uncomfortable until it becomes comfortable. That airplane that took me sky diving made me feel very uncomfortable, and the higher we climbed in the sky, the more uncomfortable I became. But only when I was willing to jump away from it was I able to discover new horizons and experience a fulfillment I never could have found by staying within the safe confines of that plane.

Reach . . . stretch . . . expand . . . jump "All in." We don't hesitate or vacillate. We don't go part way. We jump right in. We immerse ourselves in action.

Those who practice Ollin and expand their comfort zone don't approach life as spectators. They get off the sideline and start playing the game. They take control of their life. Instead of seeing themselves as thermometers, at the whim of the external environment, they see themselves as thermostats, capable of regulating and controlling the environment that surrounds them. They live the words that the American poet Ella Wheeler Wilcox wrote: "There is no chance, no destiny, no fate, that can circumvent or hinder or control the firm resolve of a determined soul."

GOING "ALL OUT" TO GO "ALL IN"

Sometimes going "All in" means *going all out*. It means exiting the pathology that keeps you imprisoned. It means taking control of your life, no matter how out of control it may seem, with firm and undaunted resolve.

No one typifies going all out better than my resilient friend Julia Stewart. She grew up in a hostile environment fueled by the relentless fighting of her parents. Her repeated attempts to remedy the situation proved futile, and police visits to her home became routine. School, a place that once served as a sanctuary, became a rumor mill of hurt and humiliation.

As home life became increasingly violent and insufferable, she decided to do something drastic before someone died. The earthquake she needed to flee was all around her, so late one night she boarded a bus and left home.

After three days of soul searching, she returned with a clearer view of the problem and successfully appealed for help for those she loved.

Though young and impressionable, Julia resolved to not let her circumstances rule her life. She determined to part company with misery and victimhood, for she knew in her heart of hearts there must be a better way. That decision changed the course of her life. She went back and finished high school. She went to work as a hostess at a local pancake house and worked her way through college. She returned to the restaurant business after college and worked up through the ranks to become one of the most revered and respected executives in her industry.

Julia is now CEO of IHOP, the parent company of that little pancake house that first employed her, and Applebee's, the largest casual dining chain in the world. Her leadership style is legendary. She is keenly aware of and responsive to her employees' needs. She knows that in life it is not what has happened to you, but what you do with what has happened. She understands how going all out can get you "All in."

Ollin is your way out. You can't overcome abuse or addiction or obesity or indebtedness without ridding yourself of it. You can't do it a little bit at a time. You have to get it all out. Whatever it might be, once you've decided on the direction you want to go, you need to commit with all your heart, might, mind, and strength.

Ollin isn't something you do part time. It isn't something you do every so often or when it's convenient. Ollin is something you practice every day of your life. It's a habit, a life habit that brings remarkable rewards. "Habit," as I learned from the Master of Words, originated from the Latin *dress*. A habit wasn't simply something you did; it was something you would hold or possess, something you wore each and every day.

IF YOU CAN'T WALK, SWIM

On the same beach trail where I like to walk and watch those passionate surfers, I rounded the corner one day and almost punched out 911 on my cell phone. I thought a drug dealer was dumping a body.

There in the salt water, where the tide meets the sand, I watched in disbelief as a man dumped a woman out of a wheelchair into the water and then retreated back to the seashore with the empty chair. But before I could do anything more, the man ran back out to where the woman was in the water, and together they began swimming out with the tide. I watched mesmerized as they swam toward the end of the San Clemente Pier, a quarter mile in the distance. Occasionally, I could see their fins come out of the water, reflecting the sun's rays.

I decided to wait until they came back to shore so I could meet them, unaware that it would be a while. For more than an hour the duo swam through the ocean's waves, lapping the end of the pier and then returning. They swam powerfully but methodically, as if they were in no hurry.

Eventually, they came back to shore, and I watched again as the man trotted on the sand to the wheelchair (it was fitted with balloon wheels) and rolled it back to the water's edge, where he met the woman, who was just finishing her swim, and just as deftly as he had deposited her into the salt water, helped her back into that chair. Then he rolled her up the beach toward the beach trail. After I walked up and introduced myself, I finally had the opportunity to hear their story.

They introduced themselves as Richard and Mary and explained that they come to this stretch of the beach to swim almost every day. The reason for the wheelchair, they explained, and Mary's rather unceremonious entry into the ocean, had to do with a diagnosis some two decades earlier when she was told she had multiple sclerosis, a disabling disease that attacks the immune system and renders muscles increasingly ineffective.

But if Mary couldn't walk very well, she could float just fine. Always a strong swimmer, it was her exercise of choice. In the ocean, her MS couldn't stop her. The tricky part was getting in the water. That's where Richard came in. He was Mary's water taxi. He explained that he and Mary had been coming to the pier area to swim for the past ten years, and he had learned how to deftly drop her into the ocean at a safe depth, then rush the chair back to the shore before returning to help orient her and swim with her around the pier.

He assured me I wasn't the first person who witnessed the unusual launching.

For Richard and Mary, the ocean swim was an important part of their life. It kept her body active and, she contended, helped keep her MS in check and her energy up. It kept Richard in touch with the woman he loved, and gave him the exercise he needed as well.

Just because a wave of life had knocked them down didn't mean they retreated to the safety of their home, closed the curtains, curled up in bed, and stayed there. They didn't become victims. They didn't submit to self-pity. "I could sit home all day and then at night cry myself to sleep," said Mary. "But I believe we each have a mission, and I wasn't going to let this deter me from fulfilling mine." Mary and Richard's answer to the challenge of multiple sclerosis wasn't to give in; it was to dive in more fully than ever. They refused to be spectators. The glow about them at the end of their daily swim reflected a satisfaction and contentment with life that comes only from those who are fully engaged.

The words "Ollin" and "passion" are two sides of the same coin. They are companions, inexorably intertwined. Together, they produce enormous results. When we decide what it is we are willing to suffer for, and what we are equally willing to act on, the world opens up. As the ancient Aztecs knew, when the earthquake hits, you have to get moving, and it has to be *now*. You have to get Ollin.

My Journal Thoughts on *Ollin*

Going "All in" means total commitment.

Ollin isn't something you do part of the time or just when you feel like it.

Dorothea Brande wrote, "All that is necessary to break the spell of inertia and frustration is this: Act as if it were impossible to fail. That is the talisman, the formula, the command of right about face which turns us from failure to success."

What would I do if I knew I couldn't fail?

What calls to me?

What energizes me?

What makes me feel I'm at my best?

What goal, idea, relationship, job, or dream makes me want to start running and jump "All in"?

What would happen if I committed to get "All in" with my marriage? My health? My career? My education? My finances? My personal relationships?

"Magnum" is a Latin word for great. "Opus" means work. What is my great work, my magnum opus?

I need to jump in with all my heart to accomplish my great work. By doing five positive things every single day toward its attainment, I can realize my goal. Imagine taking five ax swings a day at a tree. No matter how big or strong, the tree will eventually fall.

When I act as if it were impossible to fail, unseen forces come to my aid, and I develop what the Aztecs called an "Ollin heart."

IDENTIFY AND HONOR A PRACTITIONER OF
Ollin

SELECT someone you know whose behavior best reflects the principles of Ollin.

WRITE that person's name in the box provided below.

REACH OUT to and teach that person the meaning of "Ollin" and explain why he or she personifies this word.

CHAPTER ELEVEN

INTEGRITY

Living a life of integrity starts with making and keeping promises, until the whole human personality, the senses, the thinking, the feeling, and the intuition, are ultimately integrated and harmonized.

— STEPHEN R. COVEY —

I had just placed the pan of oatmeal on the stove in the kitchen when I heard the phone ringing in my office. By the time I took the call and returned, the oatmeal was burned, and the pan was charred. My eleven-year-old daughter, Sharwan, was assigned dish duty that day and shot me a worried look.

"Don't worry about that pot," I told her. "I burned it, and I will clean it. Go ahead and wash everything else, and I'll make sure that's taken care of by tonight."

The next morning Sharwan walked into my room holding the sullied pan, a bewildered look in her eyes.

"Dad, you promised me you were going to clean this up," she said. "You're writing a book about words, but you don't keep your word."

The accusation stung as only a guileless accusation can. I wondered how many times I had carelessly promised something and let the other person down. I apologized and washed the pan. Right then. I didn't wait until the next day. I did what any father caught red-handed would do: I jumped up and washed the pan—and resolved to keep my word the next time.

I clearly needed to work on my integrity.

WHOLE AND COMPLETE

Few words carry more depth of meaning than "integrity." The popular modern definition is one of being honest and having strong moral conviction, but its roots go much deeper than that. "Integrity" comes from the Latin "integer," which, as you'll recall from elementary math, refers to a whole number. Integrity of one's word means our word is *whole* and *complete*. Not just a part of our word. Not a fraction of our word. Not two-thirds, or three-fourths, or nine-tenths of our word. Not part of the time. Being whole and complete with our word entails living one hundred percent of our word, one hundred percent of the time.

Bona fide integrity is the rarest of all traits. It is not easily attained or maintained. It is a revered quality that brings extraordinary worth and value to one's life.

One of the highest compliments one can be paid is to be called "a person of complete integrity."

SINE CERA

In old Italy, unscrupulous sculptors would hide flaws in their work by filling them in with wax, thus presenting their sculptures to be what they were not. It was only a matter of time until the wax would melt or crumble away, revealing the flaw in both the work and the artist. Authentic artisans began identifying their artwork as genuine by stamping each piece with the Latin words "sine cera." "Sine" meant *without,* and "cera" connoted *wax.* A "sincere" sculpture was one made *without wax.* This stamp of authenticity gave customers confidence about their purchase.

HOLLOWNESS OR HOLINESS

When we are comfortable with who we are, we cease to be uncomfortable with who we are not. We become one with creation when we honor the promises we've made to ourselves and others. We create a life of abundance and fulfillment when we are one with our word.

When we are one with our word, we are one with the world.

The words of William Shakespeare ring with timeless resonance: "This above all: to thine own self be true; And it must follow, as the night the day, Thou canst not then be false to any man."

When we vainly attempt to deceive ourselves, we compromise and complicate who we are, and in so doing we become a fraction of what we could be.

Integrity means a life of *wholeness*. It is a completeness that brings blessings of simplicity and harmony into our lives. To "bless" is to *make holy*. Our path becomes a sacred path of holiness when we are whole. When we are not whole, our path becomes a path of hollowness. "Hollow" comes from "hole," which is the part we are left with when we take out the first letter of the word "whole." Hollow is also what we become when we choose to be only part of who we really are.

GIANT OF A MAN

One of the real giants in my life was my scoutmaster, Lester Ray Freeman. He was barely five feet tall, and although I towered over him even as a Boy Scout at twelve years of age, the sizable influence he had on my life cannot be measured with a simple ruler.

Scoutmaster Ray taught the first human development seminar I ever attended. It was not in a hotel ballroom or in a corporate boardroom; it was held in his favorite setting, the great outdoors. He showed me how to survive and take care of myself when exposed to the forces of nature. He taught me how to set a goal, how to aim for a target, how to walk along the path in the direction of my dreams, and how to help others do the same. Above all, he clearly embodied how to be content with who you are and who you were born to be.

Ray was born with disproportionate limbs—a genetic condition had caused the bones of his arms and legs to develop shorter and thicker than normal. As a result, his height was inhibited. When he was a kid, he became the object of frequent pointing and taunting. He would often seek refuge in nature. As a young boy, he would take an annual summer sojourn to the mountains to accompany his sheepherder father in tending his flock of sheep. Ray grew to love the outdoors, for the wide-open spaces renewed his spirit and restored his sense of worth. He lived the salient words of John Burroughs, "I go to Nature to be soothed and healed, and to have my senses put in order." He learned that Mother Nature, as Burroughs observed, teaches more than she preaches, and through deep observation realized that all of her creations are uniquely different, that there is no perfect mold. As he followed the flock and moved through nature, nature moved through him. A sense of belonging and unconditional acceptance swept into his soul. His sanctuary in the mountains served to teach him that nature excludes no one, and this awareness allowed him to discover his natural self, to be who he was meant to be.

Ray's yearly pilgrimage to the woods continued after he became our scoutmaster, for he intimately knew of the healing benefits of Mother Nature's touch. He knew that going outside would in fact help us each go inside; just as he had found himself in his private moments of solitude, we could similarly find ourselves.

Ray treated us Scouts with such respect and dignity that we all looked up to him as if he were ten feet tall.

He worked as a brick mason at a steel mill. His short, muscular arms were as powerful as any man's I've ever seen. His co-workers called him "Shorty," and he answered to it without rancor.

"You live with what you've got," I remember him telling us. "There's no sense crying and screaming about what you don't have. It doesn't do any good."

"I don't have long legs. Big deal," he used to say.

He'd smile and say that he was the only guy at the mill who didn't have any nicks or scratches on his hard hat.

"Be yourself; don't try to be nobody else," he would tell us. "And let it go at that. I never tried to be anybody but myself."

Ray always held the bar a little higher for me and for all the Scouts in our troop. He taught me that I could do and be more. He read somewhere that the Boy Scouts kept a ranking of the top fifty troops in America. He told us we could make that list, if we wanted it enough, and a year later our little band of misfits was the forty-seventh ranked troop in the country in our category.

BEING WHO YOU ARE

I lost track of Ray for over a quarter of a century. In the meantime, I set out on my career and started a family. One day while reflecting on the people who had the most profound impact on my life, his name was at the top of the list. I wondered if he was still alive and if I might track him down. I called information for the city he used to live in. Within seconds of receiving his phone number, I called and got his answering machine. I left a message. The next day my wife, Sherry, came sprinting up to me with the portable phone in her hand as she breathlessly said, "It's your scoutmaster, Ray Freeman, the guy you've been telling me about for the past twenty years."

I couldn't put the phone to my ear fast enough. With my heart pounding in my throat, I cleared my voice and said hello to the man who had taught me I could do things I didn't think I could do.

On the other end of the phone I heard Ray's booming voice bellow out, "Kevin Hall! How the heck are you?"

"I'm doing great, Ray," I said. "I'm so glad you called back. It's been such a long time I decided to try and track you down. Where are you living now?"

Ray responded with a roaring laugh. "Why, Kevin, my boy, I'm right where I've always been. I'm living on the same street, in the same house I've lived in for the past forty-five years!"

It was vintage Ray. He was the real deal. He hadn't

changed at all. He knew who he was and where he was.

We made arrangements to meet at his home. As I neared his residence a few days later, I found myself driving down the same road I'd biked and walked a hundred times before, and old familiar emotions welled up inside me. It was here, at Ray's home, that I'd spent countless hours working on the skills necessary to become an Eagle Scout. Memories resurfaced as I walked up the gravel driveway. I remembered Ray riding next to me in a boat, in case I froze up on my required mile swim . . . Ray checking our tents each night to make sure we were safe and sound . . . Ray taking care of me when I slammed my hand in a truck door and nearly went into shock at a high mountain campground. Neva, his wife of fifty years, greeted me at the front door and ushered me in. As I stepped inside their modest home, it struck me how much smaller it seemed compared to when I was a boy. Ray was sitting in the corner, still bigger than life, holding something in his powerful hands. He stood up and shook my hand firmly, and with a grin that went from ear to ear, he reached out and handed me a beautiful nature scene he'd carved from wood. How appropriate, I thought, that the man who knew how to carefully carve and mold the rough edges off boys was now doing the same with coarse chunks of wood.

"Here, Kevin. It's for you," he said with a twinkle in his eye.

"I can't accept that, Ray. It must have taken you hours to carve," I protested.

He cocked his head back and chortled, "Time is all I

have. It's really all I've ever had to give. Now, take this, or you'll hurt my feelings."

I humbly accepted the gift and sat down on the couch next to the wood-burning stove in his quaint family room in the home that he'd built board by board with his own two hands. Together we reminisced on his twenty-plus years as a scoutmaster. I reminded him how he would hide behind bushes and scare us and squirt us with water and wake us up in the morning growling like a bear. "It's not my fault," he protested. "I don't think I ever grew up."

He motioned me to come into the spare bedroom that doubled as his office. He opened a drawer in his desk and said, "Here are folders of every boy who came through my Scout troop." I couldn't believe it. I said, "What? You had hundreds of boys go through your troop. You've got a folder on every one?"

He answered, "I've got a folder on every boy. I recorded every goal, every advancement, every significant milestone for every single boy."

He reached far back in the stack and said, "Kevin, here's your folder." Inside was a sketch of my boyhood. Here was empirical evidence that Ray Freeman had been with me every step of the way. He knew who I was and where I needed to go and what I needed to do. He was the ultimate pathfinder. During his twenty-year tenure, he saw more than four dozen boys become Eagle Scouts, a prodigious number for any scoutmaster.

Ray Freeman taught me all I needed to know about integrity when we were Boy Scouts. He taught me about teamwork, he taught me about keeping your word, he taught me about being prepared, he taught me about problem solving and innovating together. As I left Ray's house and got in my car, he waved from the porch. His wife stood behind him, a foot taller, and just as when I was a kid I was surprised to again notice Ray's height. It was always like that. Talk to him for five minutes, and you'd never notice that he wasn't the tallest man you'd ever met. He felt tall.

I took one final look at the most complete man I've ever known and was reminded again that with people of integrity, what you see is always what you get. Ray is completely congruent being who he is. He is whole, authentic, and complete. He is integrity. It's no wonder he could see the wholeness in everyone around him.

Oscar Wilde expressed it best: "Be yourself. Everyone else is already taken."

EVERYTHING IN ITS PLACE

The Boy Scout motto is "Be prepared." The French have a similar expression, *"mise en place"* (pronounced MEEZ-ahn-PLAHS). It means *to put everything in place.* When French chefs get ready to prepare a signature dish, they don't begin until they have first assembled all the ingredients and tools that they need. The entire kitchen is organized: the spices, the correct knives, the cooking utensils, the measuring cups. They never wing it. All is measured out properly and set out in the proper order so when it is time to execute, they are ready to go. They know the importance of every element and how disastrous it can be to leave anything out.

In life, the trouble starts when we don't have ourselves and what we need to use in place. When we fail to prepare, we prepare to fail. When we go partway, cut corners, or try to get by when we know we are missing this piece or we leave out that part, we are setting ourselves up for failure.

How many shortcuts have we taken that truly saved us time? Yet the world is full of superficial promises and shortcuts. I was walking past a magazine stand and saw these headlines: "Debt-Free in 3 Months!" . . . "Lose Your Belly in Just 12 Days!" . . . "10-Day Plan to Ultimate Beauty" . . . "1 Hour to Health & Energy!" . . . "Build Wealth Fast!" A golf magazine promised, "Cure a Slice in 10 Seconds!" Such peripheral pollution is everywhere advertising the quick fix and trumpeting instant gratification. It drowns out the simple, clear, muted lessons of nature. Nature does not take shortcuts. It does not skip seasons. It does not provide instant results. We have to plant before we can harvest. There are no exceptions.

It's definitely tempting to have what we want when we want it, but it's not integrity. Integrity is the sum of all the parts, and shortcuts, by definition, do not include all the parts. Integrity is a combination of time, effort, consistency, and purpose.

A life of integrity also means taking in, accepting, and embracing the help, psychological support, and advice of others. In technology, an integrated circuit combines all the necessary components into one whole. When we connect with others and share each other's strengths, we have an integrated circuit running through our lives.

TOGETHER WE CAN DO SO MUCH

An example of what I mean by a human integrated circuit is the father-and-son team of Patrick John Hughes and Patrick Henry Hughes. I met the two Pats on the speaking circuit.

Patrick Henry Hughes was born without eyes and a tightening in his joints that prevented his limbs from straightening. Blind and crippled, there seemed little future for the boy. But when he was old enough to be propped on the piano bench in the Hughes' living room, his parents made an extraordinary discovery: the one-year-old could play tunes almost instantly after hearing them. Even more miraculous, he was playing requests a year later at the tender age of two.

Patrick and Patricia Hughes then set out on a quest to give their son every opportunity to develop his musical talents. After Patrick graduated from high school in his hometown of Louisville, Kentucky, his reputation having preceded him, the band director at the University of Louisville asked Patrick to become a member of the marching band.

Patrick was flattered to be asked to join the band but also befuddled. "I mean, how in the heck am I supposed to march?" he wanted to know.

That's where his dad stepped in.

The band director worked out an arrangement where Patrick would sit in his wheelchair and play his trumpet, and his father would wheel him around the field. They became a two-person member of the Louisville marching band. At every game they took their place in formation just like every other member of the band. The sight of what two people could accomplish acting as one was an inspiration to all. After the games, young Patrick got as many high fives from fans as the football players.

Playing in the marching band isn't the only accomplishment for Patrick. His parents have provided him as many opportunities as they could to help him find his own path and purpose. He has performed his music at arenas ranging from the Grand Ole Opry in Nashville to the Kennedy Center in Washington, D.C., and has written a book, *I Am Potential,* where he details the fulfillment that has come from expressing his gifts. "I don't have disabilities at all, just more abilities," he once told an interviewer on national television. "God made me blind and unable to walk. Big deal. He gave me the musical gifts I have and the great opportunity to meet new people."

The Hughes family exemplifies the power and strength that develop when the various parts of a unit, in their case a family unit, come together to produce something that otherwise wouldn't be possible at all. Helen Keller, who traveled a similar path as young Patrick so many years before, acknowledged that "alone we can do so little; together we can do so much."

It is remarkable what happens when a group galvanizes for a common cause. I've witnessed a dramatic example of this when an associate of mine in the hospitality industry, Billy Shore, formed an organization of restaurateurs around the country. Collectively, they set out on a mission to begin to put an end to childhood hunger. Each night in America and around the world millions of children go to bed hungry. It was a lofty and formidable challenge. But these business leaders knew that there are great quantities of food that go to waste every day in their own industry. So they devised a plan to take their surplus food and distribute it to children in need. In addition, they organized "Taste of the Nation" events to use their combined culinary skills to raise funds to buy more food to distribute to the needy. In the first four years, Share Our Strength has served more than forty million meals to hungry children. Every year since, the number has kept growing. Billy knew he couldn't do much alone, but by connecting with others, millions of children have been fed who otherwise would have gone to bed hungry.

AN INTEGRAL TEAM

Our path is not meant to be traveled alone. In previous chapters we've talked much about the importance of recognizing people on our path who appear to help us find and fulfill our purpose. Identify these key pathfinders and develop them into a personal board of advisors who can be consulted for direction and guidance. The talents, strengths, and experience of these advisors can often make our weaknesses and inexperience irrelevant because they help us focus on our strengths.

Napoleon Hill taught that "people take on the nature and the habits and the power of thought of those with whom they associate in a spirit of sympathy and harmony . . . No two minds ever come together without thereby creating a third, invisible, intangible force which may be likened to a third mind."

We can start at the top of the learning curve and establish personal power in our lives as we reach out to those on our personal board of advisors and ask them to help us identify and develop our unique strengths. They will call forth insights, suggestions, and plans to help us achieve our goals and definite purpose in life.

Creating an integral team means surrounding ourselves with people who are growing, improving, learning, and making a difference. The entrepreneur and renowned speaker Jim Rohn reminds us that "we are the average of the five people we spend the most time with."

When strengths are integrated, the whole of the team is always going to be greater than the sum of its parts, which is the ultimate definition of synergy. Amazing things happen when everyone contributes.

My Journal Thoughts on *Integrity*

Ralph Waldo Emerson said, "I cannot find language of sufficient energy to convey my sense of the sacredness of private integrity."

"Sacred" comes from the Latin "sacrare," which means to <u>consecrate and make holy</u>.

"Private" comes from the Latin "privatus," which means <u>belonging to oneself</u>.

A life of true integrity encompasses the private and the sacred. Wholeness and holiness become my ever-present companions.

I have a noble purpose: I choose to live each day with excellence.

Thomas Edison said, "If we did all the things we are capable of doing, we would literally astound ourselves."

It's time to start astounding!

It's time to start fulfilling my potential!

It's time to start living with purpose!

IDENTIFY AND HONOR A PERSON OF

Integrity

SELECT someone you know who personifies Integrity.

WRITE that person's name in the box provided below.

REACH OUT to and teach that person the meaning of "Integrity" and explain why he or she personifies this word.

A CONCLUDING

Afternoon with Arthur

I had something I couldn't wait to show Arthur. It represented the last four and a half years of my life, a journey that began quite unexpectedly and without warning on the streets of Vienna. There, in the heart of Europe, a wise man from India taught me about Genshai, what I would call a secret word, for it sent me in search of secrets in other words and of those who could help me discover the secret power of words.

It was that search that brought me to this wise, effervescent Master of Words, who showed me that there are words that help us get on our path.

I reached in my briefcase and removed a large sheaf of papers. It was my manuscript. It contained the eleven words that headline the chapters of this book: Genshai. Pathfinder. Namasté. Passion. Sapere Vedere. Humility. Inspire. Empathy. Coach. Ollin. Integrity.

Each word I had discussed with Arthur, and each word he had amplified with his remarkable wisdom and insight.

With his large hands he reached out for the package, a childlike look of curiosity on his weathered face. A present of words! For Arthur it was Christmas morning.

He turned past the title page and began to read the opening chapter. "Oh," he said, "this is wonderful. I can't wait to read all of it. I will begin tonight. Thank you, Kevin."

I was grateful that he would, yet also apprehensive. It's a humbling thing, giving a book about words to the undisputed Master of Words.

I started into my disclaimer, "It's rough and I know there are mistakes . . . ," but Arthur waved his hand as he continued to stare at the manuscript.

"I'm sure it's fine," he said. "I'm sure you've done your best work."

As I sat there in Arthur's single room—a room that, after ninety-three years of such a rich, varied, and well-traveled life, now easily housed all of his worldly possessions—I reflected on the unerring kindness and patience Arthur always exhibited. Even when I was running late, which was most of the time, he was the picture of grace and acceptance. I realized his life story was reflected in the words of this book.

Genshai. *Never treat anyone small.* From his fellow residents at Summerfield Manor to all his guests and family and friends, he treats no one in a manner that would make them feel small. He makes you feel as if you are the most important person in the room.

Pathfinder. *Leader.* As surely as if his ear is literally on the ground, he unfailingly reads the signs and clues that reveal the secret power of words.

Namasté. *Saluting the Divine within.* Every day he focuses on doing what he uniquely does best.

Passion. *Suffering for what you love most.* He loves words, and he loves his family, and he spends his life willingly suffering for them both.

Sapere Vedere. *Knowing how to see.* Even at his advanced age, with poor hearing and fading eyesight, his insight remains 20-20.

Humility. *Being coachable and teachable.* He knows countless words in multiple languages, yet he tapes a new one on the mirror to learn every single day.

Inspire. *Breathing life into another.* Every time I enter his room, he breathes life into me and my dreams.

Empathy. *Walking the path of another.* Through his love of language and his fellow man, his ability to relate to others knows no boundaries.

Coach. *Carrying another.* With his regular Thursday afternoon "Culture Capsules," he carries his fellow residents around the world.

Ollin. *Moving forward with all your heart.* All his life he has taken his gifts and jumped "All in."

Integrity. *Whole and complete.* His whole life's work reflects completeness.

I stole a look at Arthur as he continued to leaf through the manuscript. I realized that words would be forever transformed in my mind thanks to the illuminating wisdom of my master teacher. I realized that Arthur is truly one of the great gifts in my life.

I reached into my bag and produced another book— my pathfinder journal.

"I would be honored to have you sign this," I said, thrusting toward him my Book of Greats.

Without hesitating, he took my pen and signed his name.

The Master of Words

The masters in the art of living make little distinction between their work and their play, their labor and their leisure, their minds and their bodies, their information, their recreation, their love and their religion. They hardly know which is which; they simply pursue their vision of excellence at whatever they do, leaving others to decide whether they are working or playing.

— JAMES A. MICHENER —

The Book of Greats

At the end of each of the eleven chapters in this book you have listed those people who personify the word identified in that chapter. Now use those names to start your own personal Book of Greats—a register of those individuals who have enriched your life.

Honor and recognize them by having them sign next to the word that represents them.

You will see additional pages for new names, for your Book of Greats is not yet full. Others will appear to help you discover your path and fulfill your purpose. Add them when they do.

Remember, it is all a journey.

The Book of Greats

Master of Words _Arthur R. Watkins_

Genshai

Pathfinder

Namasté

Passion

Sapere Vedere

The Book of Greats

~

Humility _____

Inspire _____

Empathy _____

Coach _____

Ollin _____

Integrity _____

The Book of Greats

The Book of Greats

Kevin's Book of Greats

I express profound gratitude to all the "greats" who have appeared on my path and have influenced this book.

To Pravin Cherkoori for sharing with me a secret word that releases human potential, and Professor Arthur Watkins for sharing the secrets of all words.

To Richard Paul Evans, Spencer Johnson, MD, and Jeff Flamm for your keen insights on the book's title and subtitle; Lee Benson for bringing my thoughts and insights out of the clouds and onto the written page (your skill, patience, humor, and hard work made this book a reality); Margret McBride, the world's greatest agent, for recommending the "Afternoons with Arthur" and "My Journal Thoughts" sections—you personify excellence; and to Donna DeGutis, Faye Atchison, and Anne Bomke at the Margret McBride Literary Agency for your mastery of your craft; Mary Ellen O'Neill, the finest editor an author could ever have, for catching the vision of the book; Liate Stehlik, a world-class publisher; Michael Morrison, for believing in the book's message; Iskra Johnson, for your exquisite calligraphy; Laura "Eagle Eye" Daly, copy editor extraordinaire; Dennis Webb, my Power of Words business partner, for your unwavering support; David Jobe, for creating a deadline and platform to launch the first printing of the book; Michael Hall, for your unconditional assistance, kindness, and administrative excellence; Fran Platt for your masterful design layout and painstaking effort; Bill "Print Broker" Ruesch for thinking and acting out of the box; Brad Airmet, at FC

Printing, for making the impossible possible; and Jackie Guibord and Mary Hill for your countless hours of volunteer proofing of words . . . and words . . . and more words. You were heroic!

I would also like to thank early readers and advisors Cindy Andra, Modesto Alcala, Raylene Anderson, Ty Bennett, Dave Blanchard, Steve Carlston, Alice Elliot, Jerry Johnson, Blanch Linton, Joan Linton, Gilbert Melott, Dan McCormick, Patti Miles, Peter Miles, Edna Morris, Pat Murphy, Bill Peterson, Barry Rellaford, Judy Schiffman, Lance Schiffman, Marlene Siskel, Jeff Smith, Philip Webb, and Martsie Webb for your invaluable feedback and insights.

And to everyone who has influenced my personal path and purpose, especially Ray Freeman and Larry Hall for the early direction that changed the course of my life; Stephen R. Covey for modeling a life of integrity; Norman Brinker for personifying humility, empathy, and—above all—Genshai; James Newman for "rejoicing in my success" and connecting me to Viktor Frankl and the Statue of Responsibility project; and Viktor Frankl, Og Mandino, and William Danforth for putting in writing words that lifted and inspired me.

To my mother, who convinced me I could do anything I dreamed; to Sherry—you are the love of my life— thank you for always believing in me, and may the next thirty years be as sweet as the last; to my children and grandchildren—your lives make me proud.

To my Creator—for every gift and every word.

AfterWord

By Dr. Gerald Bell,
founder of the Bell Leadership Institute

Kevin Hall has created for us in this marvelous book a path we can take to seek higher levels of contribution by being more effective humans. Our paths may have crossed that remarkable day in the Grand Tetons because we are both passionate about helping others find meaning and significance in their lives. Kevin's path involved getting people (including twelve-year-old Scouts) to set their goals and purposes as early as they can, then helping them acquire knowledge and skills to keep at it and achieve those aspirations. My path led me to what I call "The Study of 4,000," where thousands of older individuals looked back on their lives and lamented letting life unfold without creating a plan of what they wanted to do. They regretted the randomness of lives shaped by external stimuli rather than internal goals and focus.

People tend to think their lives will be rigid if they have a purpose, but just the opposite is true. If they set goals, it will set them free. This has been confirmed time and time again over the course of the past thirty-five years as I have taught over 500,000 leaders in more than 4,700 organizations, from over eighty-five countries, in the specifics of leadership and goal achievement. Kevin has detailed within the pages of this book how to take control of, and master, the direction of your life. You know it now as "pathfinding." This insightful book will help you become a true pathfinder. It will help you discover and follow your unique path and purpose in life. It will teach you how to make meaningful and profound life contributions. And most important, it will be your guide to living a life with no regrets.

But you have to do more than just read it. You must act on it. It has been said, "To know and not do is to not know." I strongly encourage you to return again to the "Journal Thoughts" at the end of each chapter and consider putting those principles into action in your daily life.

You began the journey of this book with a secret word that empowers you to build yourself first. You end the journey with the challenge of becoming whole and complete. Commit wholly to growing and building a complete you, and I promise that you will contribute more than your wildest dreams.

I am so glad that Kevin appeared on my path. His love for words is inspiring. The essential beauty of words captivates him. His ability to take a word, hold it up, look at it from all sides, turn it around, listen to its sounds, state its opposite, and discover what it meant to our forebears has given you the extraordinary gift you now hold in your hands.

I believe Kevin's love for words is born out of his love for people. In his life's journey he's naturally moved toward people, embraced them, studied them, sought their ideas, and attempted to understand them. I am convinced that this original source of energy led him to the discovery of the essential centerpiece of words in shaping our lives. His passion for purposeful living is contagious. It is what brought us together in the first place.

May your path be filled with abundance and fulfillment. And if you are ever out for an invigorating summer run in the Grand Tetons, keep your eyes wide open, for that professor running your way might just be me.

— Gerald Bell

empathy
humility
PATHFINDER
Coach
ENSHAI
INSPIRE
Passion
humility
Coach
Ollín
INTEGRITY